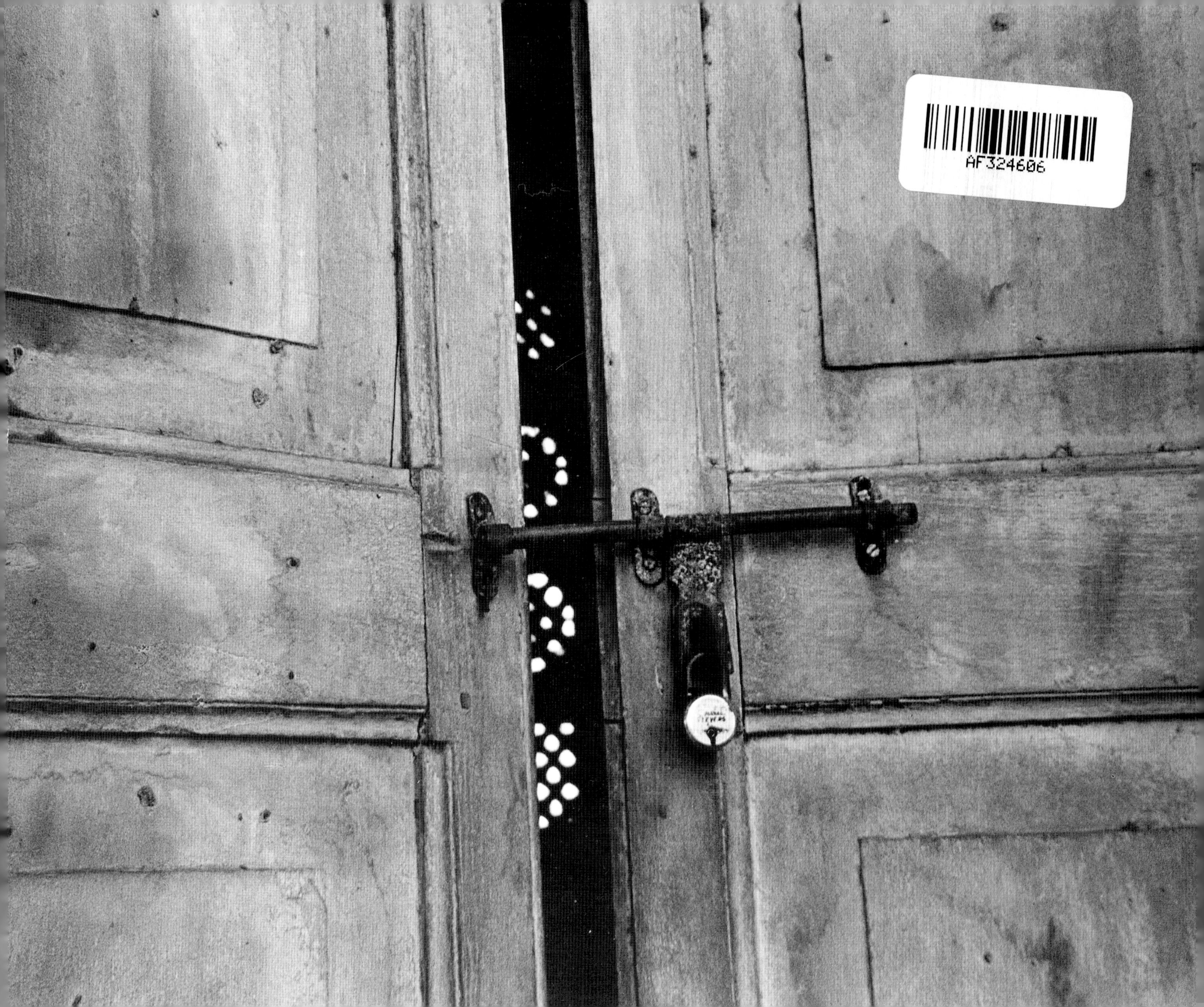
AF324606

The Getty Conservation Institute

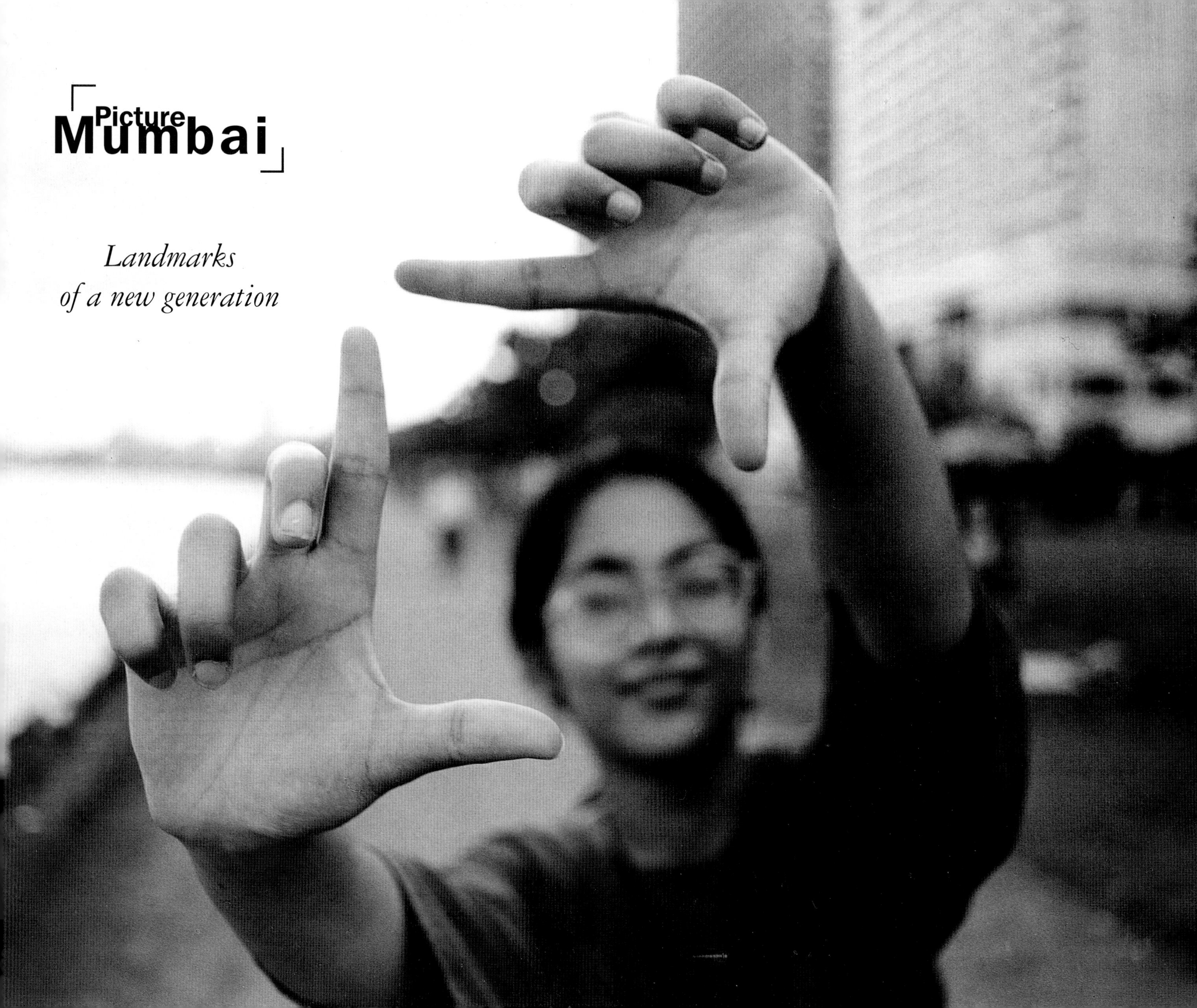
Picture
Mumbai

Landmarks
of a new generation

COVER PHOTO
Nicole D'Souza
Backbay Reclamation,
Cuffe Parade.

INSIDE FRONT COVER PHOTO
David de Souza
Koli Woman.

HALF TITLE PHOTO
Anitha Balachandran
Behind Prince of Wales Museum,
Dubash Marg.

PAGE 107 PHOTO
Sachin Chitale
Nariman Point, Marine Drive.

PAGE 118 PHOTO
David de Souza
Warehouses, P. D'Mello Road.

INSIDE BACK COVER PHOTO
Vernon Fernandes
Chowpatti, Girgaum.

BACK COVER PHOTO
David de Souza
Sachivalaya Bus Depot, J. Tata Road.

Library of Congress Cataloging-in-Publication Data

Picture Mumbai : landmarks of a new generation.
        p.   cm.
     ISBN 0-89236-464-5
       1. Architecture–India–Bombay–Pictorial works–Exhibitions.
2. Child photographers–India–Bombay–Exhibitions.
3. Bombay (India)–Pictorial works–Exhibitions. 4. Bombay (India)–
Buildings, structures, etc.–Pictorial works–Exhibitions.
I. Getty Conservation Institute.
DS486.B7P48   1997
954' .7923–dc21   96-48666
                                                        CIP
                                                         AC

This book is published in conjunction with
"Picture Mumbai: Landmarks of a New Generation,"
an exhibition organised by the Getty Conservation Institute
in collaboration with the Prince of Wales Museum of Western India
in Mumbai, which opened at the Museum on 20 January, 1997.

The Getty Conservation Institute works internationally to further the appreciation and preservation of the world's cultural heritage for the enrichment and use of present and future generations.

The Institute conducts interdisciplinary research in conservation and applies its findings to archaeological sites and monuments, historic cities, and objects and collections.

Embracing a vision consistent with the challenges of the next millennium, the Institute creates alliances for conservation; explores new ideas and approaches in the field; disseminates information to the profession and the public worldwide; and promotes community involvement in safeguarding the world's cultural heritage.

The Institute is an operating program of the J. Paul Getty Trust, a Los Angeles-based non-profit organisation dedicated to the visual arts and culture.

CONTENTS

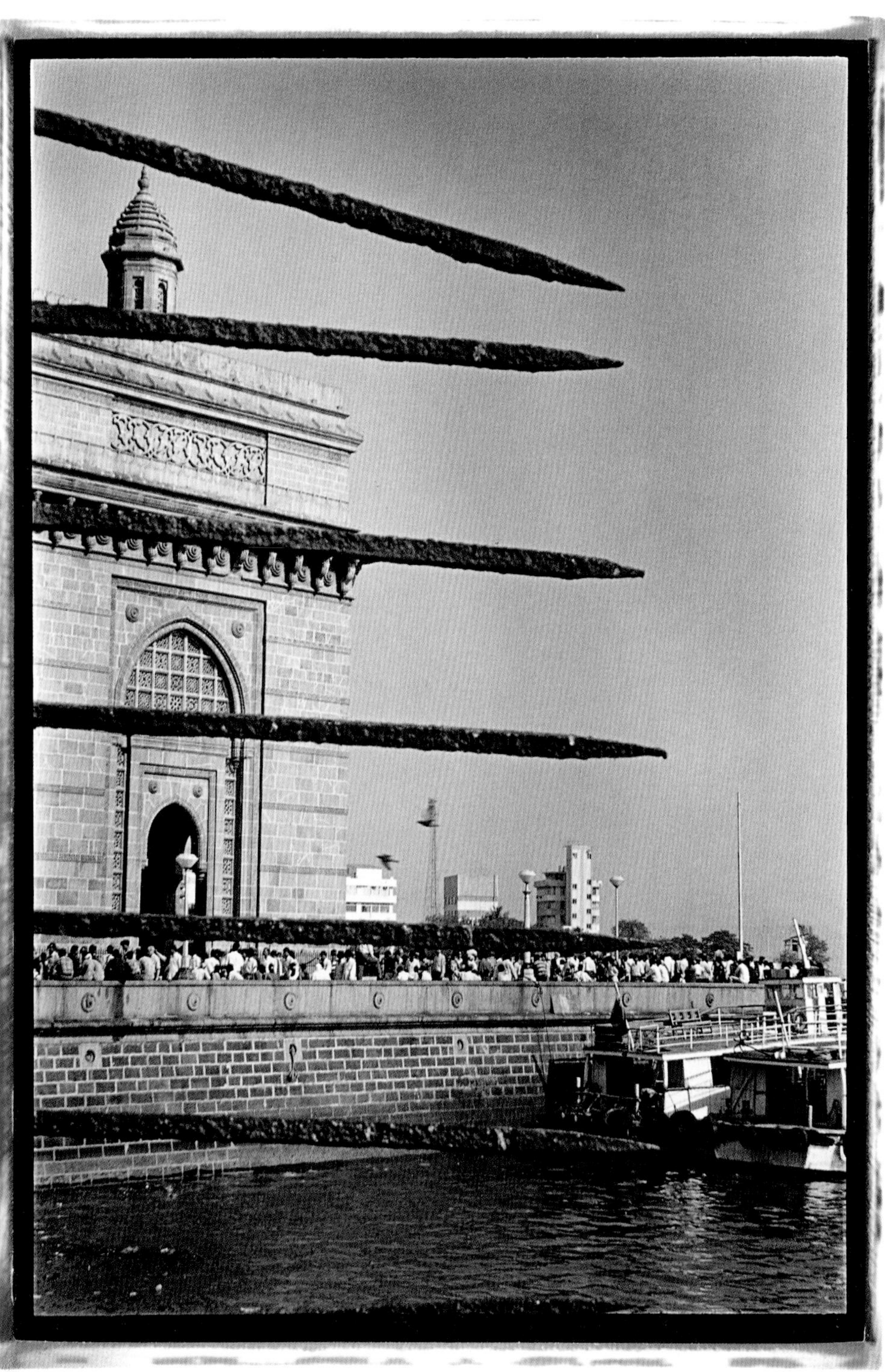

Vernon Fernandes
Gateway of India, Mumbai Harbour.

In an age of instant communications and of constant bombardments of images, how can one hope to convey what is relevant or what is important? "Picture Mumbai" can do it. It reflects the quest of a group of young people to convey what is relevant and significant for them, in their city, in today's world.

LANDMARKS

"Picture Mumbai" had its origins in a project that we, at the Getty Conservation Institute, organised in Los Angeles in 1993-94. We had commissioned a series of studies about the meaning of landmarks and the experts had provided us with respectable and acceptable definitions. But how would we convey these meanings to the younger generation in whom we had set our sights as future defenders and stewards of the cultural heritage? At any rate, what was a landmark? For some person it might represent a hill or a flagpole. For another nothing less than the Gateway of India would suffice. For some it might be the neighbourhood market and yet for others nothing short of the Taj Mahal would qualify. Who was

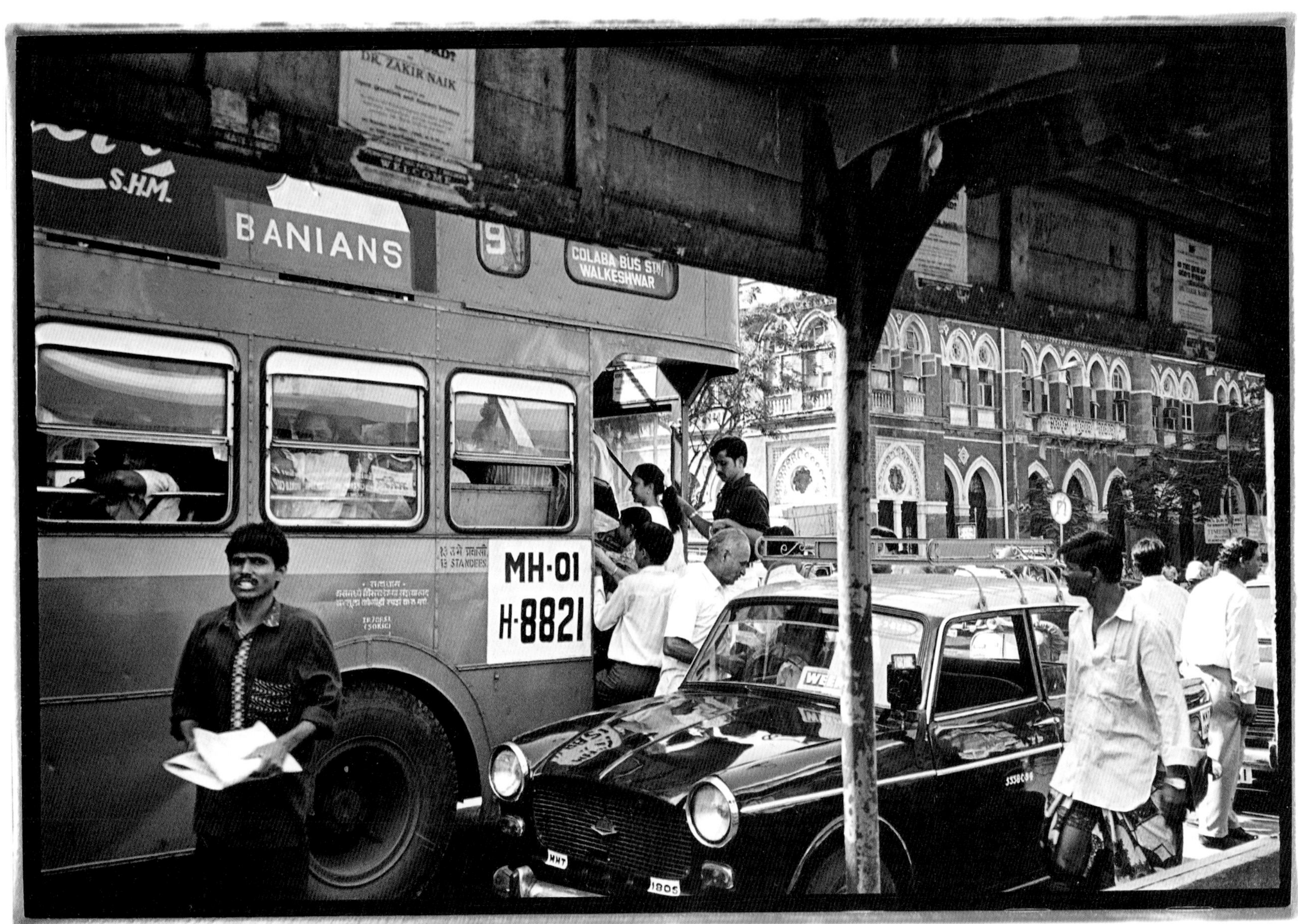

Nicole D'Souza
Next to petrol station, Colaba Causeway, Colaba.

right? Who could really say what a landmark is? I thought young people would be able to tell us about the role that landmarks play in expressing, forming, or enriching their lives and that in the process of telling us both sides would learn from each other and significantly improve the chances of the world's cultural heritage surviving in the future.

And tell us they did. Eight young people produced the images and words of "Picture L.A. : Landmarks of a New Generation." The project made us understand better our city and look at it through different eyes.

Armed with their cameras, their eyes, and their intelligence, the young photographers whose work you will see in the following pages have roamed the streets of Mumbai looking for the opportunity to tell all of us what a landmark is; what is important to them in their lives; and, in the greater context, what they hope will not be lost in the future. The images you are about to see reflect not so much a physical location as a sensation, a definition, a feeling, a hope. Sometimes they also reflect the unrelenting, incisive, objective reality. This is well, because the freshness of their minds and the honesty of their souls provide a challenge to the generation that preceded them. Are we up to these young people's expectations to provide them with the future we expect them to protect?

"Picture Mumbai" is part of the "Landmarks" campaign that the Getty Conservation Institute has undertaken in several cities around the world. Los Angeles was the first one, followed by Cape Town in South Africa, and now by Mumbai. Others will come. The success of "Picture L.A." set the tone for these projects. We have followed the same methodology in all places because youth is universal and will always rise to a good challenge. We selected Mumbai because it provided innumerable opportunities of bringing together diverse young people in a common endeavour; we were fascinated by the insightful exercise of their minds and feelings; and also because their smiles struggled to hide, but not quite, the seriousness of their purpose.

The "Landmarks" campaign has evoked for me my own youth. I remember, as a young boy, staring at monuments and sites in my native Mexico and wondering how they happened to be there. I also remember other landmarks of my young age that I now wish development and urban growth had not destroyed. There seems to be, in all of this, a continuity of reflection that not only encompasses a wide range of ages and of geographical areas but a depth of feeling not bounded by real or imagined barriers.

My thanks go to all who participated in the project: Our young photographers Anitha, Asir, Bikram, Nicole, Nivedita, Sachin, Vernon, Vinit, and Yamini; our good partner Anil Rao, who took this project under his wing and has given us unrelenting support; David de Souza, who took the arduous first steps to guide the team, as well as the arduous last steps, and in the process has given all of us so much; project assistants Nuzhat, Suresh, and Sachin; Sunil Mahadik, who reproduced their work in this handsome book; Director Kalpana Desai, who graciously accommodated the exhibition at the Prince of Wales Museum; Vinod Daniel, a former fellow at the Getty Conservation Institute and a good friend who, with pride, showed us his country and pointed us in the right direction. I wish to thank also Mahasti Afshar who has directed the "Landmarks" campaign from the start. She is permanently enthusiastic, excited, committed, and a source of inspiration for our partners in this project. "Picture Mumbai" has a special place in her heart. To her and to all—my deepest appreciation.

I am amazed at this collection of images. They elicit admiration and surprise because these young people became photographers in the process of explaining their landmarks to us. And excellent photographers at that. They are not shy, they are not blatant. They are serious, careful observers with aesthetic eyes and reflective minds; and they have captured the richness and variety of Mumbai including the concerns and hopes that young people have for their city, their neighbourhood, their surroundings, their life, their intimacy, their beliefs. I see here the youth of Mumbai hard at work, dedicated to a project that would make anyone proud. An intense and devoted youth, eager to learn and willing to give. Let us share in their vision and understanding and the joy that is "Picture Mumbai."

Miguel Angel Corzo
Director
The Getty Conservation Institute

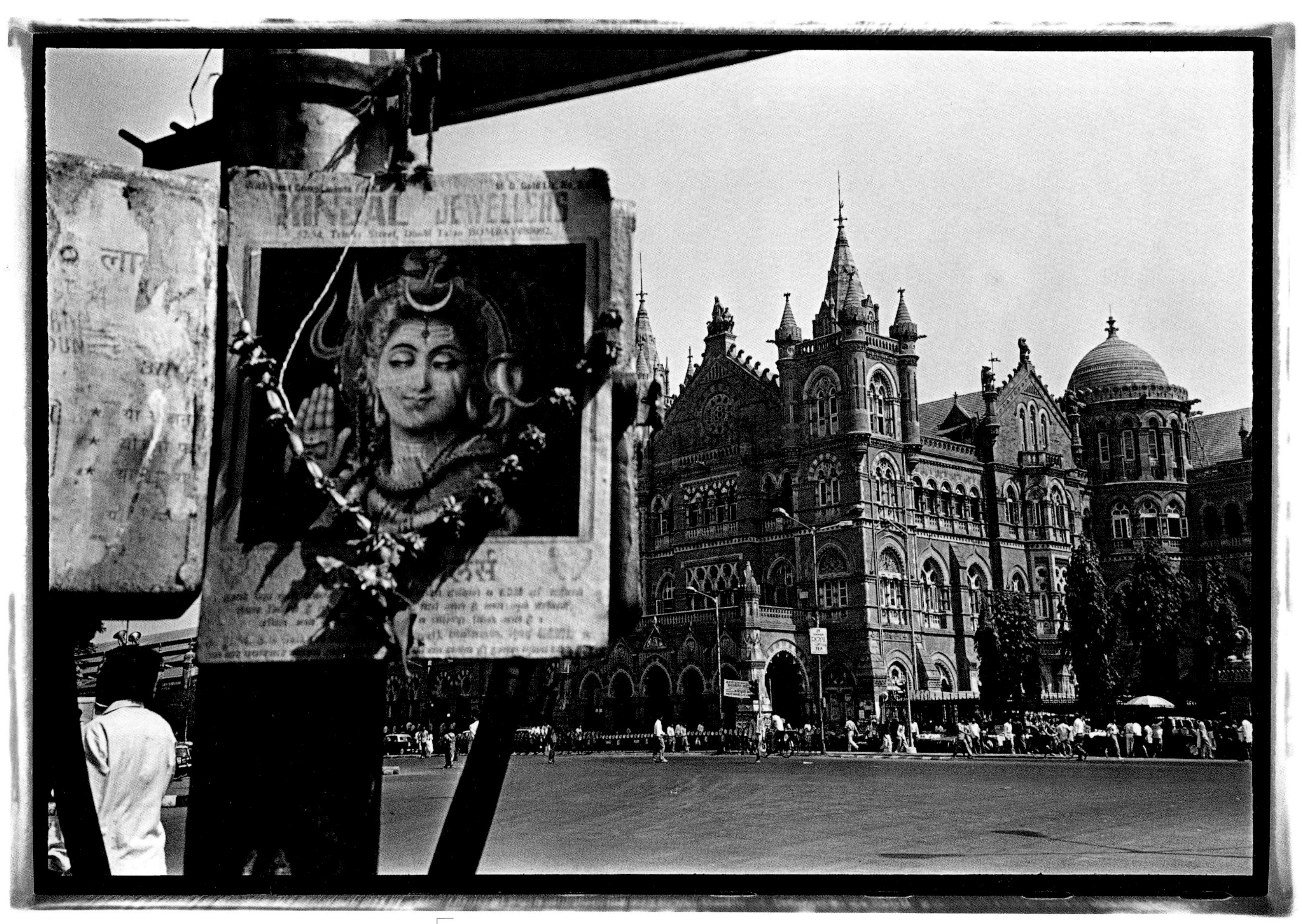

Vinit Chauhan
Chatrapati Shivaji Terminus (Victoria Terminus),
Dadabhai Navroji Road.

The original Koli inhabitants of Mumbai were almost certainly not consulted in 1661 when the King of Portugal bequeathed their seven islands as dowry in a politically correct marriage, before political correctness was the lingua franca.

Four centuries later in a democratic redressal nine young people representing Mumbai the metropolis, are gifting the city back to its citizens in a landmark visual statement.

The success of "Picture L.A.", the Getty Conservation Institute's introspective project, has snowballed into other international cities defining "Landmarks of a New Generation".

In these days of global handshakes how did the GCI choose their cities? Mahasti Afshar, a Persian with her doctorate in Sanskrit, set her sight on India early on. Why? "Because India is the birthplace of so many artistic and intellectual traditions that spread beyond its own borders across the East; and because it has refused to give up this multilayered heritage for thousands of years." Mahasti visited Delhi first, one of two cities on the GCI's short list. When she came to Mumbai we went for a drive around the city with Anil Rao who was to become the project's local patron and honorary manager. She could recognize the etymology of most of the words written in various Indian and Arabic scripts and felt she would break into Hindi if only she could stay on for a week. Mumbai's diversity and

GENESIS

PICTURE MUMBAI

vibrancy were pitted against Delhi's monumental architecture, parks, and broad avenues. In the end she went with her gut. Delhi's loss was our gain.

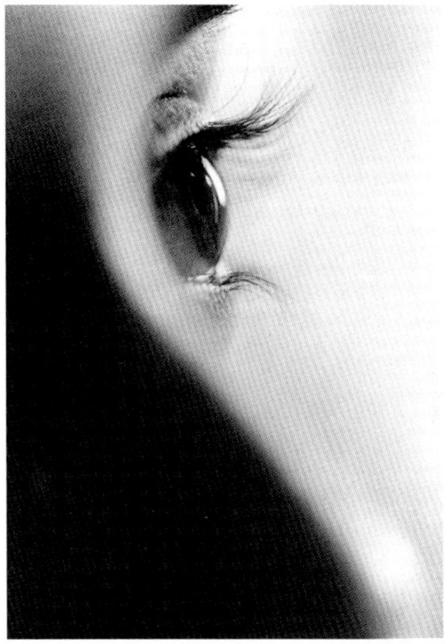

When I was handed a sealed copy of the "Picture L.A." catalogue and asked to run "Picture Mumbai", I felt very honoured, then I floated home, opened the shrink wrap, and almost suffered a cardiac infarction. The photographs were stunning, honest, real, and absorbing. I would have been proud if they were mine and this was the work of eight youngsters between the ages of ten and eighteen. I was sweating, worried, and very doubtful that I could deliver.

Photography, with auto everything cameras, was chosen as the ideal vehicle of expression. Then I set out to schools, colleges, and voluntary organisations to find nine young people. The response from principals and deans was, in the main, extremely encouraging. Ideas on the selection process presented themselves as I went along. I was acutely aware that I would have to work on the assumption that none of our young people would have any photographic experience and that, whatever I did in the interviews that followed, I would be testing their verbal skills when in fact I was looking for a visual sensibility.

Nuzhat accompanied me on several of the interviews and even arranged for some group meetings.

Anitha Balachandran
Behind Rhythm House,
Dr. V. B. Gandhi Marg.

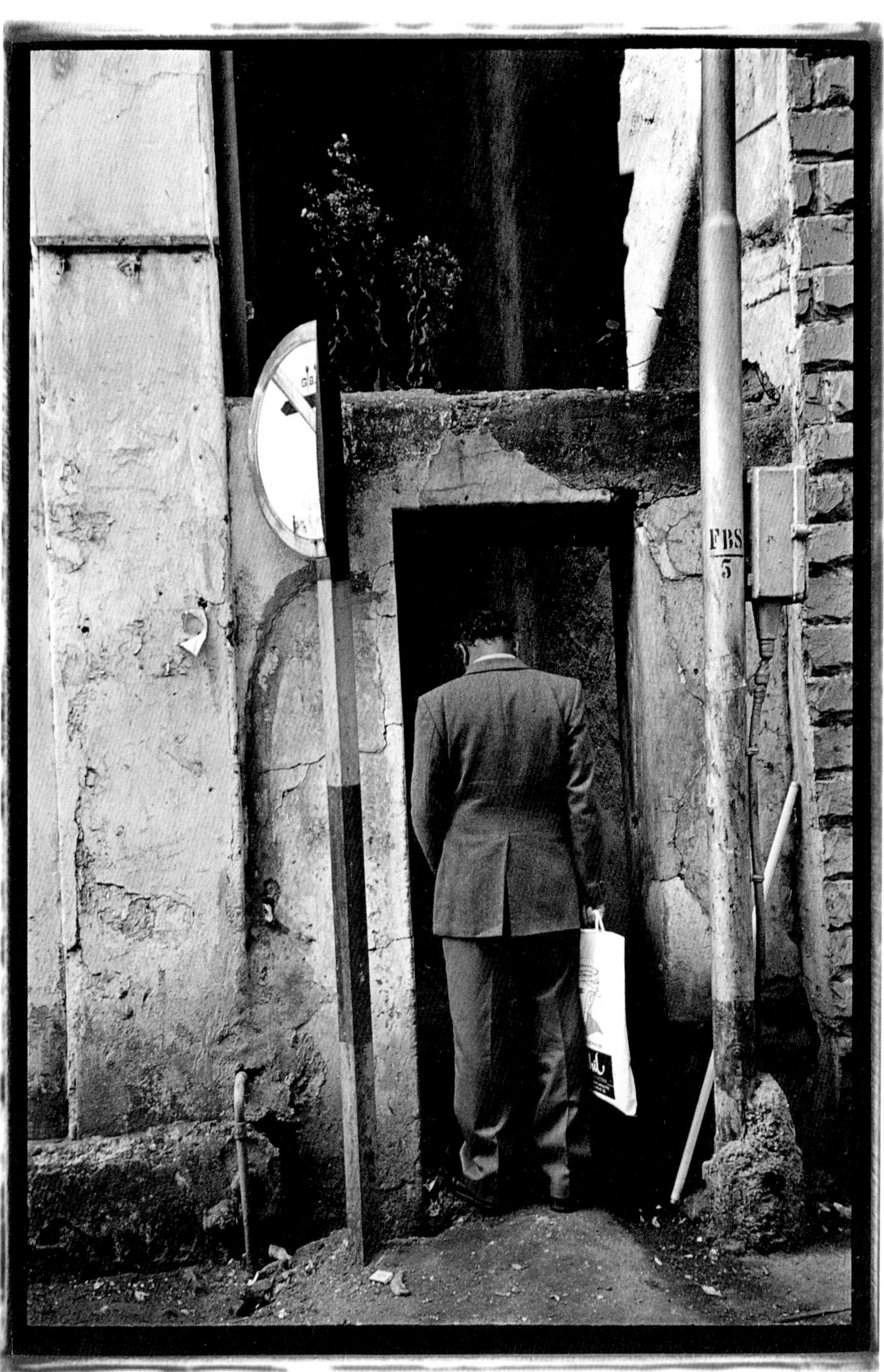

After interviewing a few hundred young people from a cross section of social, economic, and geographical backgrounds it was becoming patently clear that if the young people were self confident, and had passion with a modicum of artistic merit, they could be given a direction and a mission. I was at this stage still having sleepless nights and making inquiries into alternative accommodation had I to leave town!

Asir Mulla is twelve years going on sixty. He is a born leader, can hold a conversation with anyone, anywhere, has a wonderful home base, and plugs in there for all sorts of support.

Vernon Fernandes is a typical Bandra twelve year old. His teachers in school and his parents at home tried to warn me off by telling me of his mischief, not knowing that in fact they were, in my eyes, strengthening his case. He camouflages his intelligence under a baseball cap that is welded backwards integrating him with a worldwide rap brotherhood.

Sachin Sawant is fifteen years old, lives in Lalbaug, is quiet, observant, and treads a narrow path of fulfilling his mother's ambitions for him during this SSC examination and giving us his time for the photography that ran concurrent.

Yamini Hule is a gorgeous fifteen year old also at the tenuous SSC stage while the project was on. When I met up with her father and asked whether he had apprehensions about his daughter giving us her time at this crucial exam stage, it was incredible to hear him say that she could appear for the exam six months later in October. He was very keen that Yamini get exposed to as many new things as possible. She lives in Dadar, has numerous interests, and is full of the joy of living.

Bikram Mitra is fifteen. He is the only youngster in the group who experimented on his own making light streaks, and gathering material for a still life, table-top representation of what Mumbai means to him. He built his own enlarger and developed some of his photographs himself. He too had

this balancing act with the ICSC examination and all the usual tensions that are too familiar with any Mumbai resident, indeed, any Indian.

Anitha Balachandran is seventeen. She lives at Nariman Point. She does not take the city for granted, looks at the obvious as a newcomer, is not jaded, loves the city, is bright, and has a wonderful sense of humour. She is bemused by the satire apparent in the city and is ready to comment on it.

Vinit Chauhan is seventeen. He lives in a half-way home for runaway children in Mulund. He too is a relative newcomer to the city, is artistic and ambitious.

Nivedita Magar is eighteen, intelligent, communicative, interactive, and concerned. She has an opinion and presents it. She reads and reflects. She wonders what she is going to do with her college education and would rather be designing jewellery.

Nicole D'Souza is eighteen. She speaks her mind, is affectionate, gregarious, a party animal, and knows everyone in Mumbai. She is constantly battling her parents on curfew time. She is involved in a hundred different projects.

Since young people in our schools are given few liberties, I felt that the cameras and film should be given to them with very basic, how-to-load-hold-and-operate-the-camera type of instructions and they should be allowed to go berserk on an unsuspecting Mumbai. These nine pairs of eyes in four groups chaperoned by three adults and myself fanned out in four directions. This was to repeat itself every weekend from January 1 to March 30, 1996. Every Saturday we would all group at my place and study the contact sheets and work prints. The initial contact sheets were terrible. We would have group discussions on what went wrong and what could be done to improve the visuals, and fundamental issues arose on Landscape, Landmarks, People, Portraits. What is Significant, Important, Necessary, Ugly, Beautiful. Asir kept me straight, forcing me to trip between Marathi,

Hindi, and English 'papads' as he called it. In exchange he appointed himself the honorary professor of linguistics, corrected my grammar, and increased my vocab.

I did not show any of the young people "Picture L.A.", not wanting to give them a bias and condition their viewpoint. I did however introduce them from time to time to the photographic masters and restricted all the work to black and white only because the conversion of the real world colour to shades of grey was posing an abstract problem to some of the young photographers. For instance, one of the girls was excitedly awaiting her contact sheets of sadhus and was disappointed at the result. In colour a troupe of saffron coloured holy men could have looked great; in black and white the photograph did not pop. Soon the metaphors were beginning to translate and the images were talking. In the darkroom while making the work prints I would have on Def Leppard's Hysteria *or Dire Straits'* Industrial Disease *or Bhimsen and I'd be dancing to the harmonics of black and white. What joy! The images were showing a fantastic insight and honesty. It was beginning to work.*

I noticed also a strange transformation in attitude. While at the interview stage I must have heard a million young people talk of garbage, so much so that whenever I went to a new school I had to tell them after introduction that they could tell me of anything they considered a landmark, except garbage. Now here were these young photographers given every licence to document garbage and half way through the project none of them had. I did remind them, too. I suspect they were discovering that there was more to Mumbai than meets the eye.

I did not put any restrictions on the consumption of film for the first two months; everything was too new and marvellous to curtail. What was emerging was a landmark of humanism. This is perhaps unsurprising in a city where privacy is a luxury, where a large section of the population lives it's "private" life on the outside. The young people were seeing humans and human activity in the streets as landmarks. People marked the land. Was this enough? These questions the young people began answering themselves. Some of them wanted to include architectural details to give their landmarks a sense of location, time, and space, and set about it in their own unique way. The accompanying adults, Nuzhat, Suresh, and Sachin were fantastic; they were there and not there. The idea was to free the young people from any kind of concern except the ones related to the project. They provided all the backup in terms of transport, lunch, and thousands of Cokes and Pepsis and when we were feeling green it was coconut water and sugarcane juice. Everyone got to work with everyone; language, social status, and religion made no barrier whatsoever.

Each of the young people had their own styles. Yamini was wonderful at art directing her photographs. If she felt that this set of people would make an impact in that part of the building, she would go about explaining the project to the people and get them to suspend all work and move to the right location. Vinit would slink away and find some very unusual way of seeing the prosaic.

Asir would stop an eighty-year-old man on a bicycle and, short of making him do cartwheels, would get him to do anything he wished. I was amazed at the approach and memorised some of this stuff for my own work. Imitation is the highest form of flattery. I believe that the young people had innocent charm and were disarmingly direct. No adult could think of refusing a 'chintu' Asir.

Nivedita would take her "grab shot" then begin working the image. Invariably the last image would work best. Bikram was becoming aware that his telephoto was tending to make portraits and that a combination of his normal lens and his feet would work best.

Sachin was a master of framing the perfect picture, you would find him in some yogic contortion behind a fence, gate, or wheel, filling the vacant foreground.

Nicole has this talent to make images of lone persons in a fifteen million and counting city. She is fascinated by reflections, making surreal statements. Vernon has this ability to confuse the familiar. Anitha has a unique perception in documenting the quirks of Mumbai.

About halfway through I could identify people by their contact sheets. And yet I had to caution them from forming styles and getting stuck in grooves.

It was not smooth going all the way. Anyone with an ounce of authority would want to flex it. Wake up Mumbai, what's this "permission" thing that everyone is hung up with? Our accompanying adults were smothered by this "have you taken permission?" mantra, which invariably was rhetorical because the person who could give permission was never around or in the unlikely event that they were present, permission was never given.

It's not like some top secret nuke installation was being photographed but rather public domain, visible-from-the-main-road kind of stuff. The other chauvinistic side to Mumbai was the difference in the way Nuzhat, as a woman, was treated vis-à-vis Suresh, Sachin, or myself.

Halfway through the project Anil thought it a good idea to pre-empt parental anxiety by having a small exhibition of the work produced, so that parents would know exactly what their children were up to during the weekends. We had sixty people in my studio, including the three fixed taxi drivers who were by now totally involved in the project themselves. The one hundred odd photographs were mounted, and each young photographer introduced their work and the other photographers to their parents, who were shocked at the talent and the representation of Mumbai. The cracks in the wall, the falling apart gates, and street scenes were all recognisably familiar. The visuals have a strange alchemy in that they invoke a sense of smell that is distinctly Mumbai.

Mumbai and the young photographers both have given generously. I asked for ninety and they delivered one hundred and eighty, I got ambitious and asked them for two hundred, they delivered three hundred.

I continued to be greedy, ever seeking the levelling-off point. I have been uplifted, moved, revitalised at the vast, seething, potential in this surprising, tired old city and more importantly at the humanity exemplified by these fantastic nine young persons. I still have sleepless nights now wondering about nine times one thousand young people there waiting to be given a voice, a project, a direction, and a mission.

Mumbai the city IS. You can love it, hate it, curse it, glorify it. It allows all people to be themselves regardless of their social, political, economic, and religious status. In that sense it's a generous city, tired, aging, and very forgiving. It's home. The nine represent the Mumbai of the future, mature human beings with a sense of worth. They have inspired me with their energy, commitment, and generosity, most of all though with their honesty. I look forward to the future.

David de Souza

Field Director

THE IMAGES

A landmark shows us the way so that we don't get lost. Vinit Chauhan

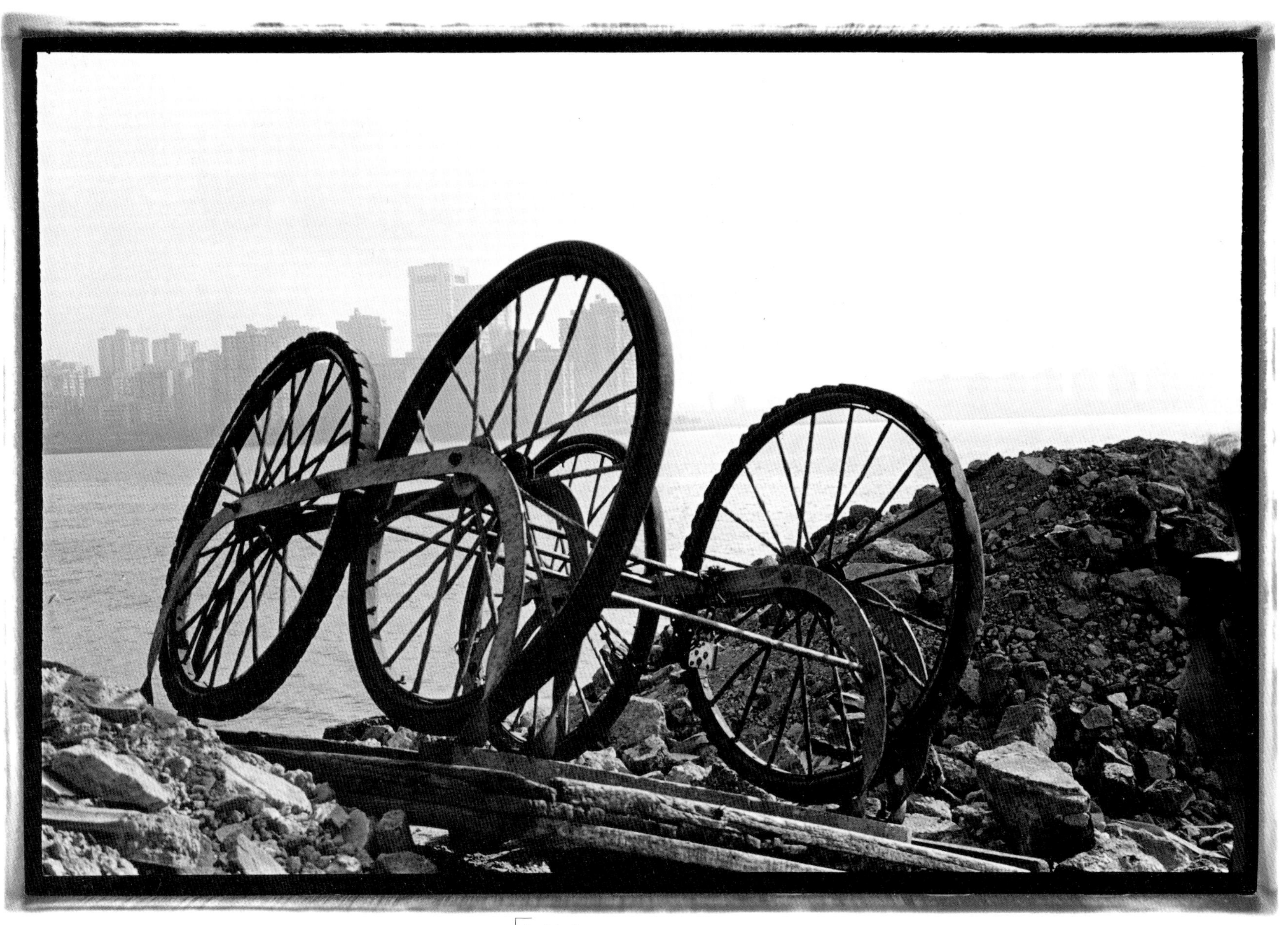

Sachin Sawant
Nariman Point, Marine Drive.

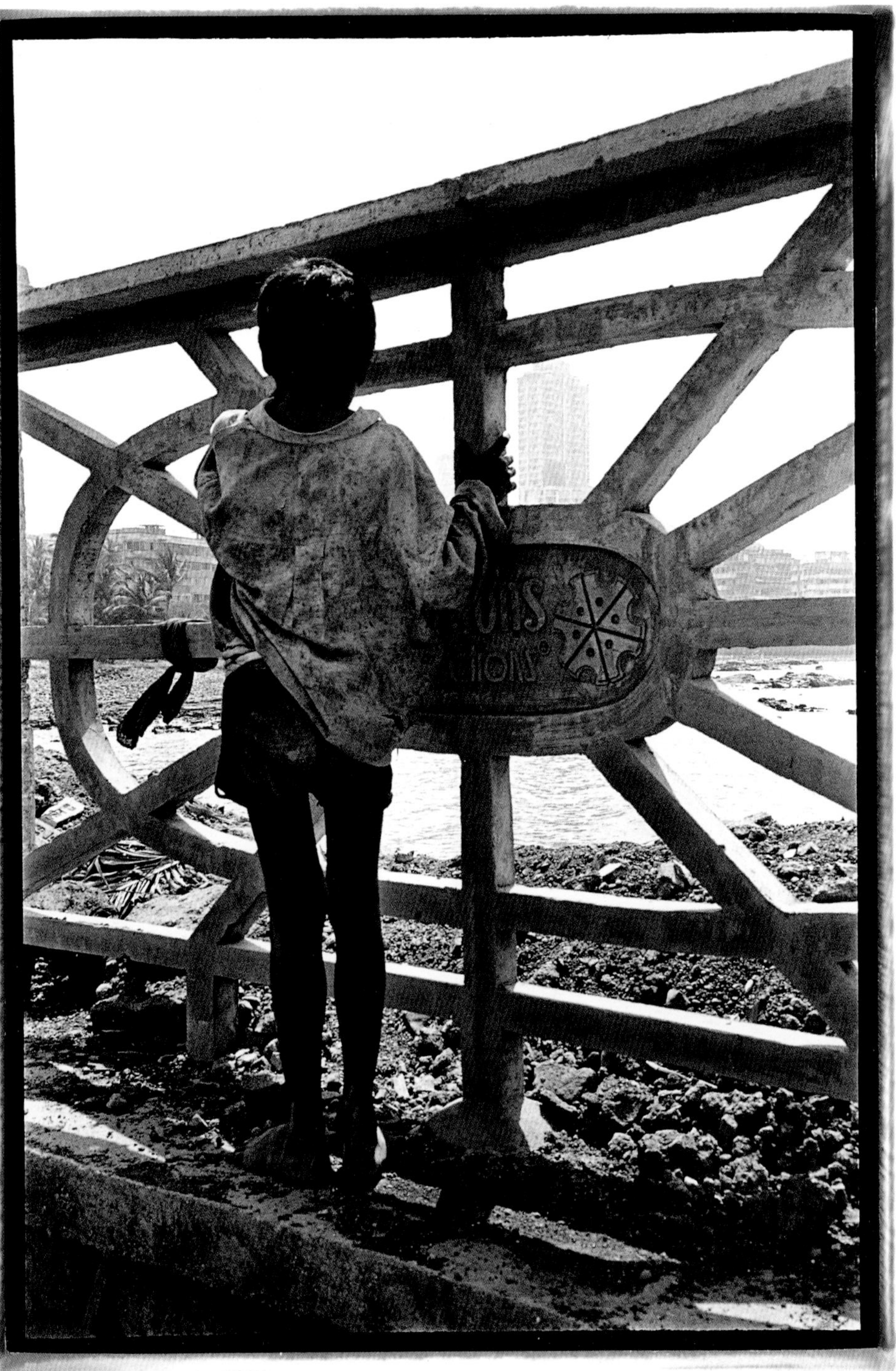

Yamini Hule
Breach Candy, Bhulabhai Desai Road.

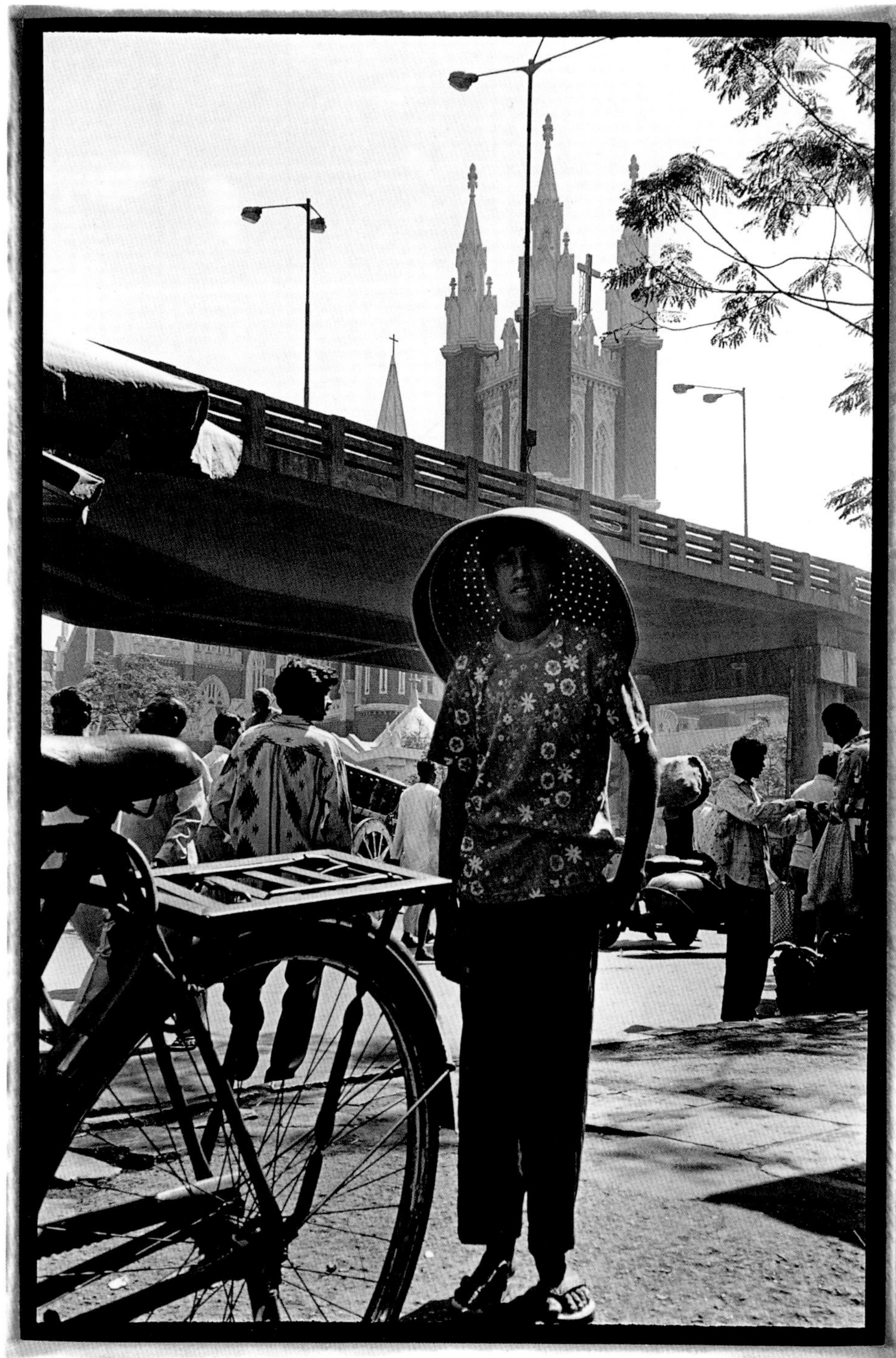

Yamini Hule
Gloria Church,
Dr. Babasaheb Ambedkar Road, Byculla.

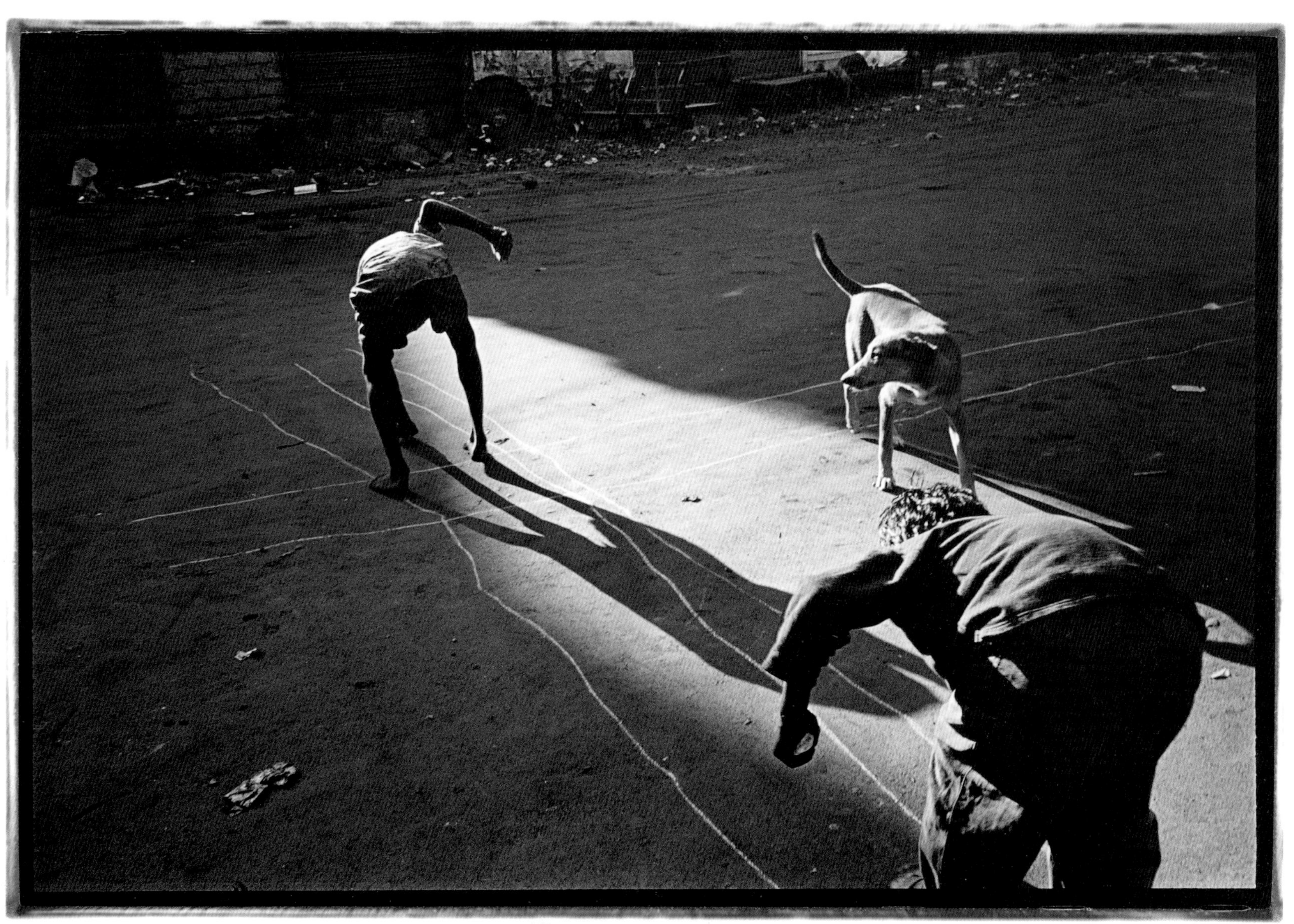

Anitha Balachandran
Dalal Street, Fort.

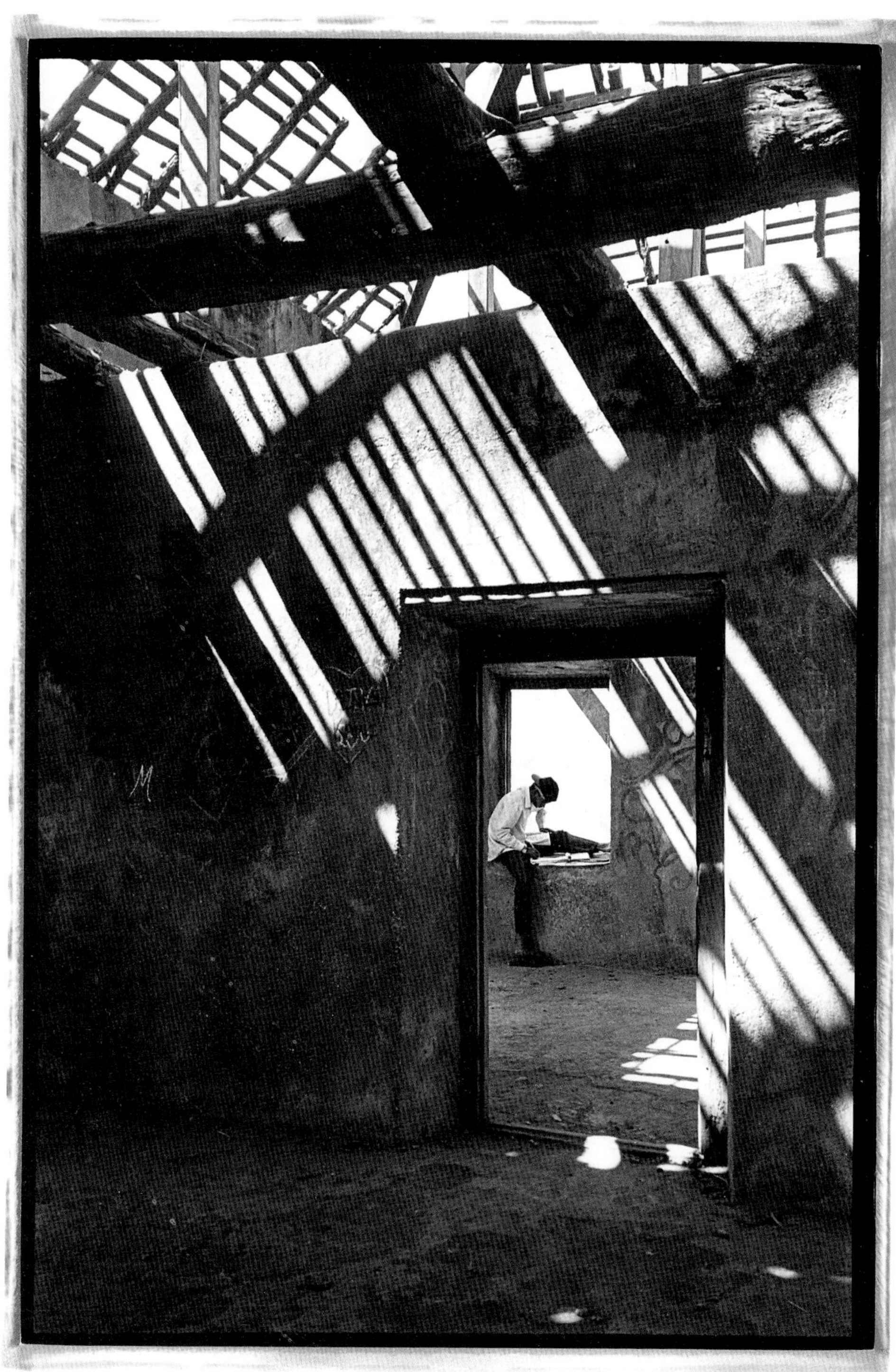

Vinit Chauhan
Sion Fort, Eastern Express Highway.

Like Rushdie's churning sea of stories, Mumbai is a whirligig of colours, smells, and sounds— one rushing into the other.

A landmark to me is something that jumps at you from this uncontrollable chaos as sense and structure.

However, it needn't be a solid structure, permanent and unflinching. Often what makes a landmark so special is the masses conveyed in that magical transiency, or the transiency itself.

Nivedita Magar

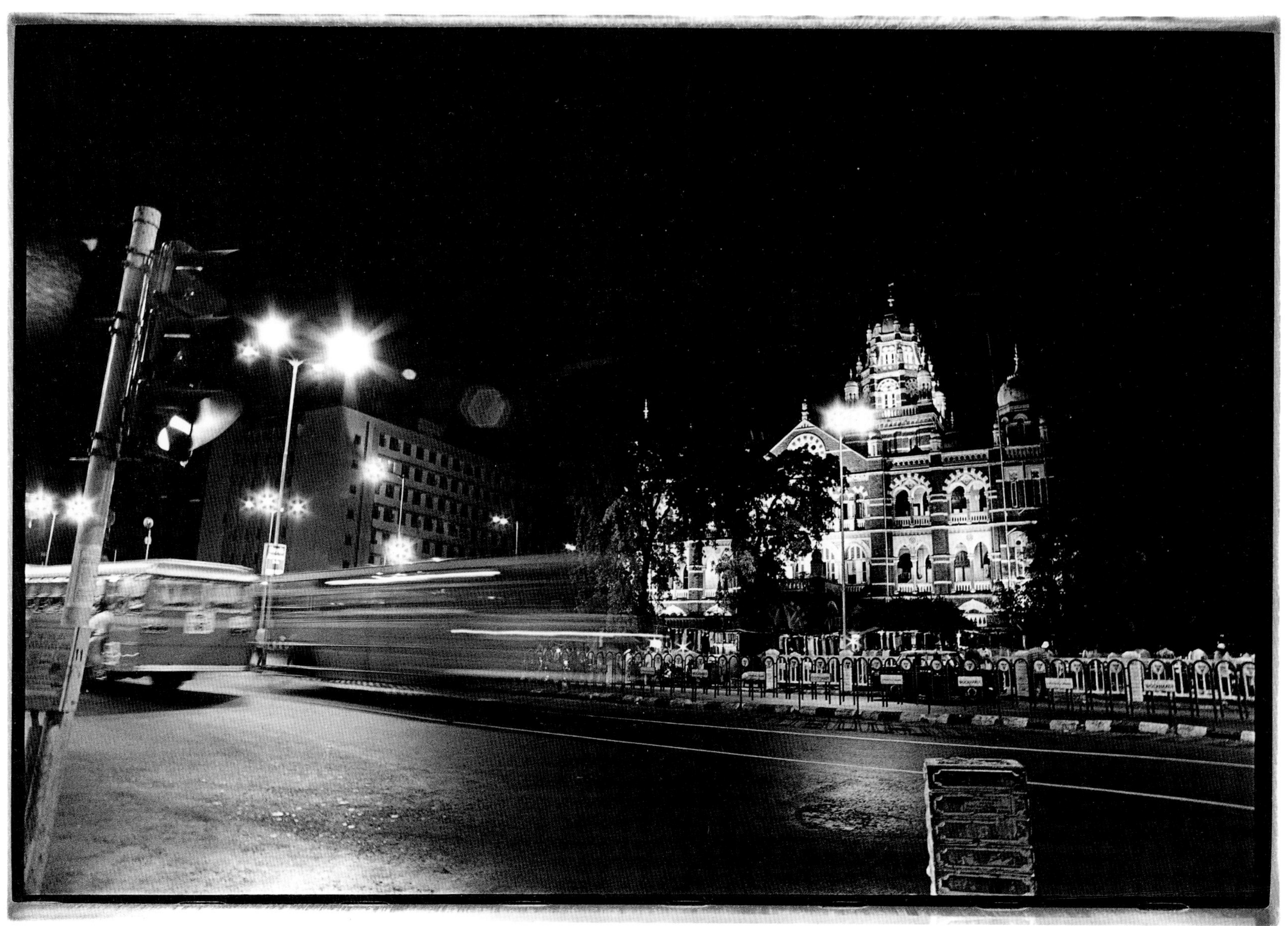

Bikram Mitra
Western Railway Office, Veer Nariman Road, Churchgate.

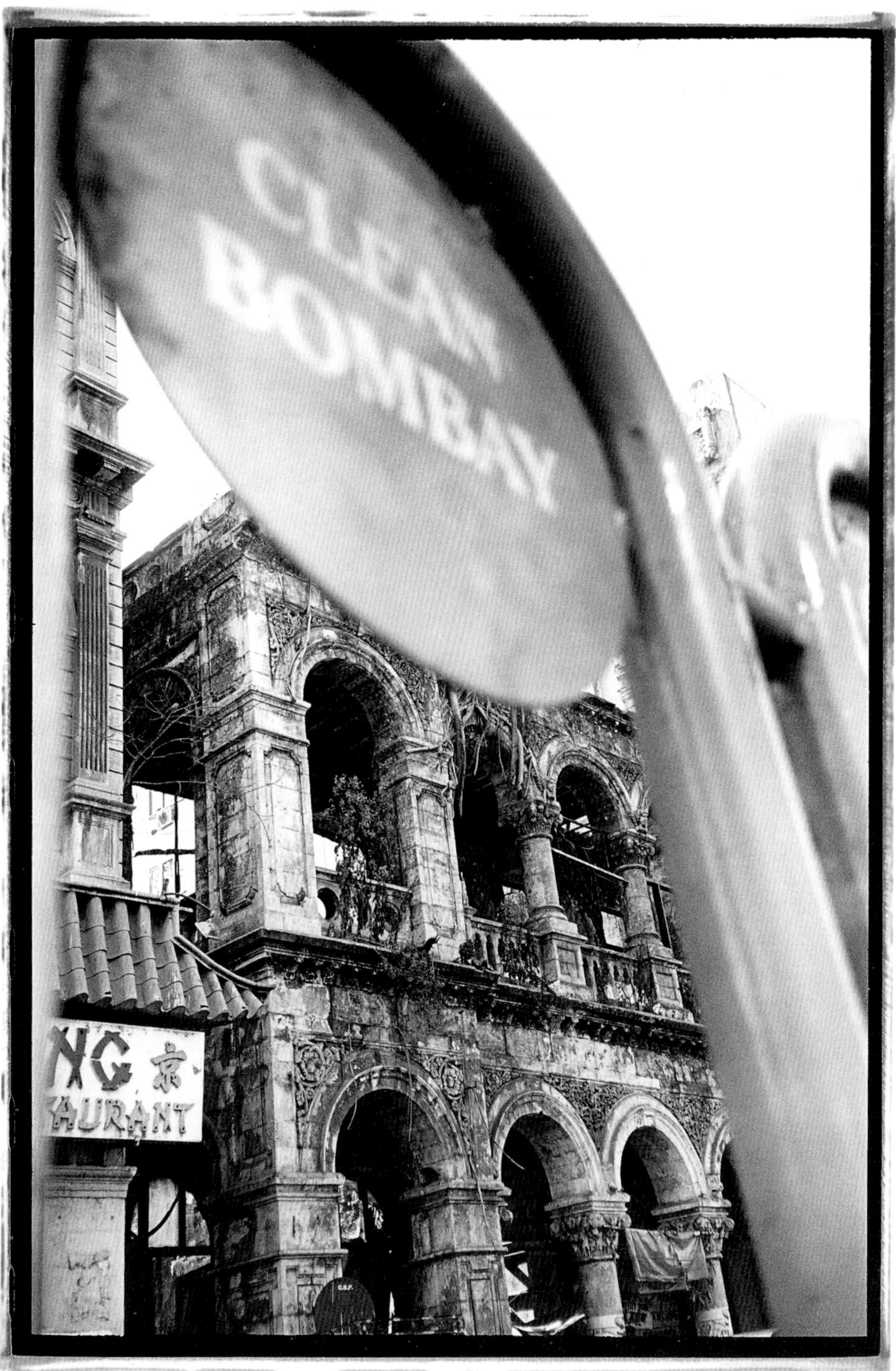

Nivedita Magar
Nanking Restaurant,
Shivaji Maharaj Marg.

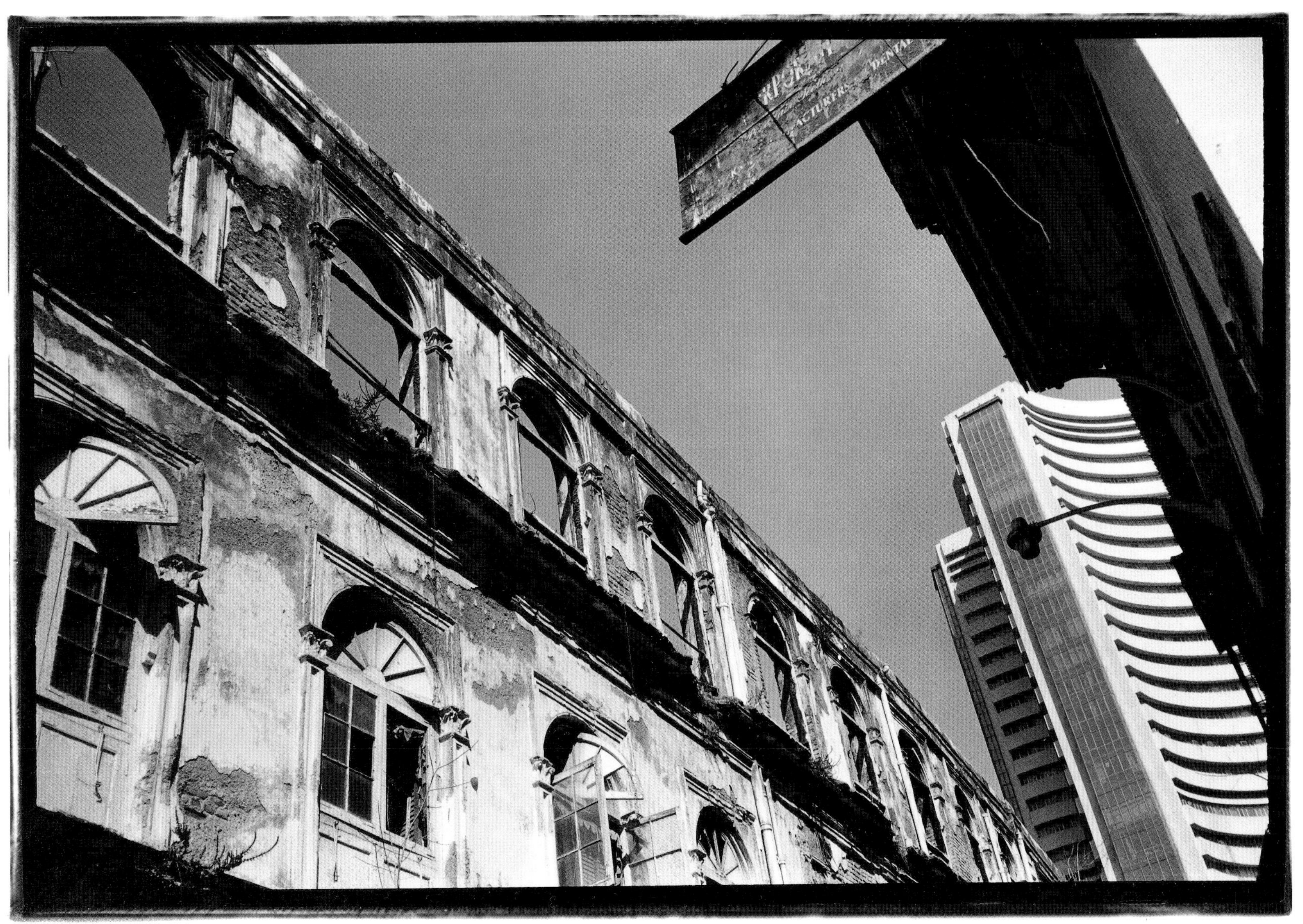

Nivedita Magar
Stock Market, Mahatma Gandhi Road, Fort.

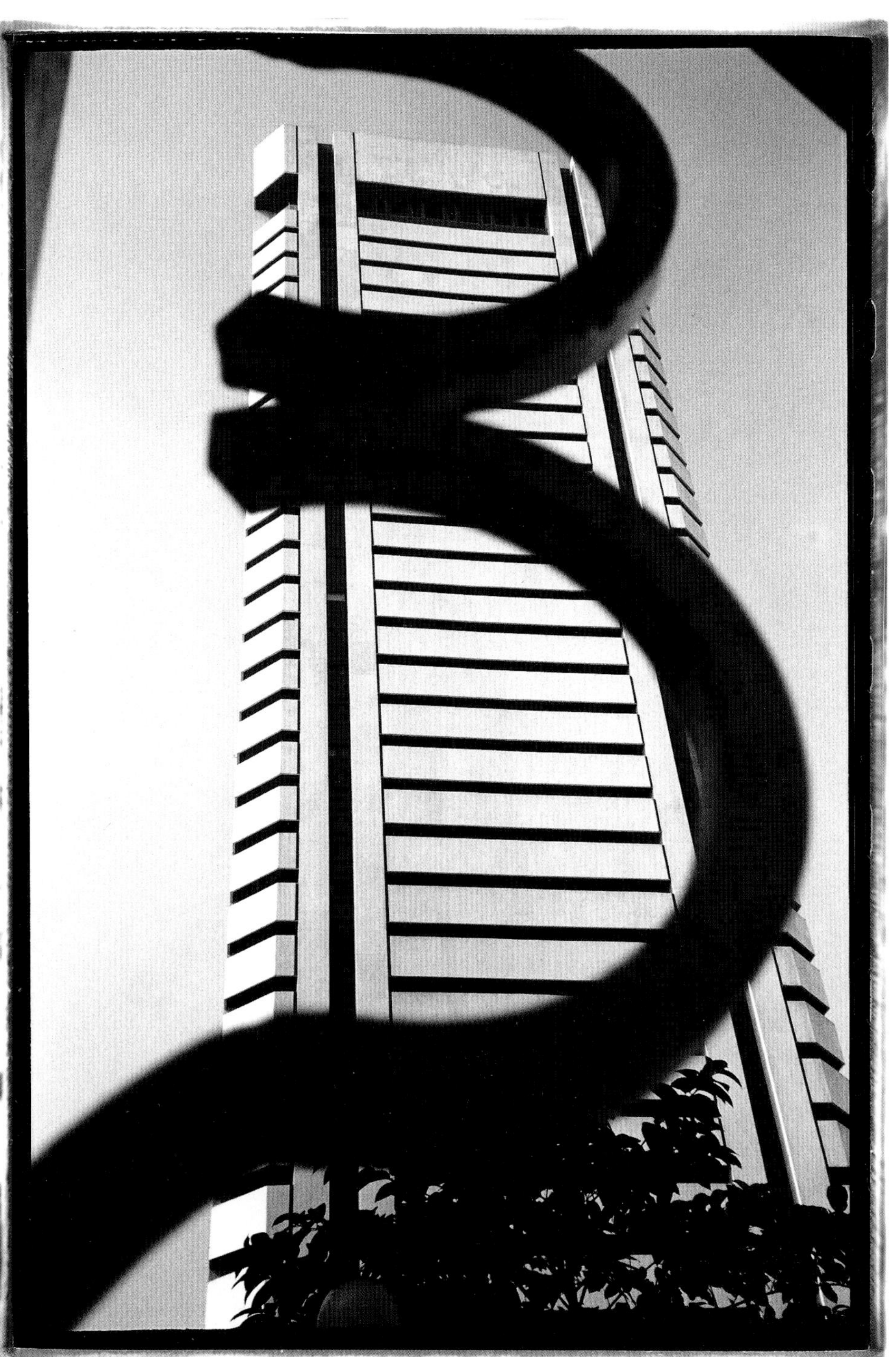

Yamini Hule

*Industrial Development Bank of India,
Cuffe Parade.*

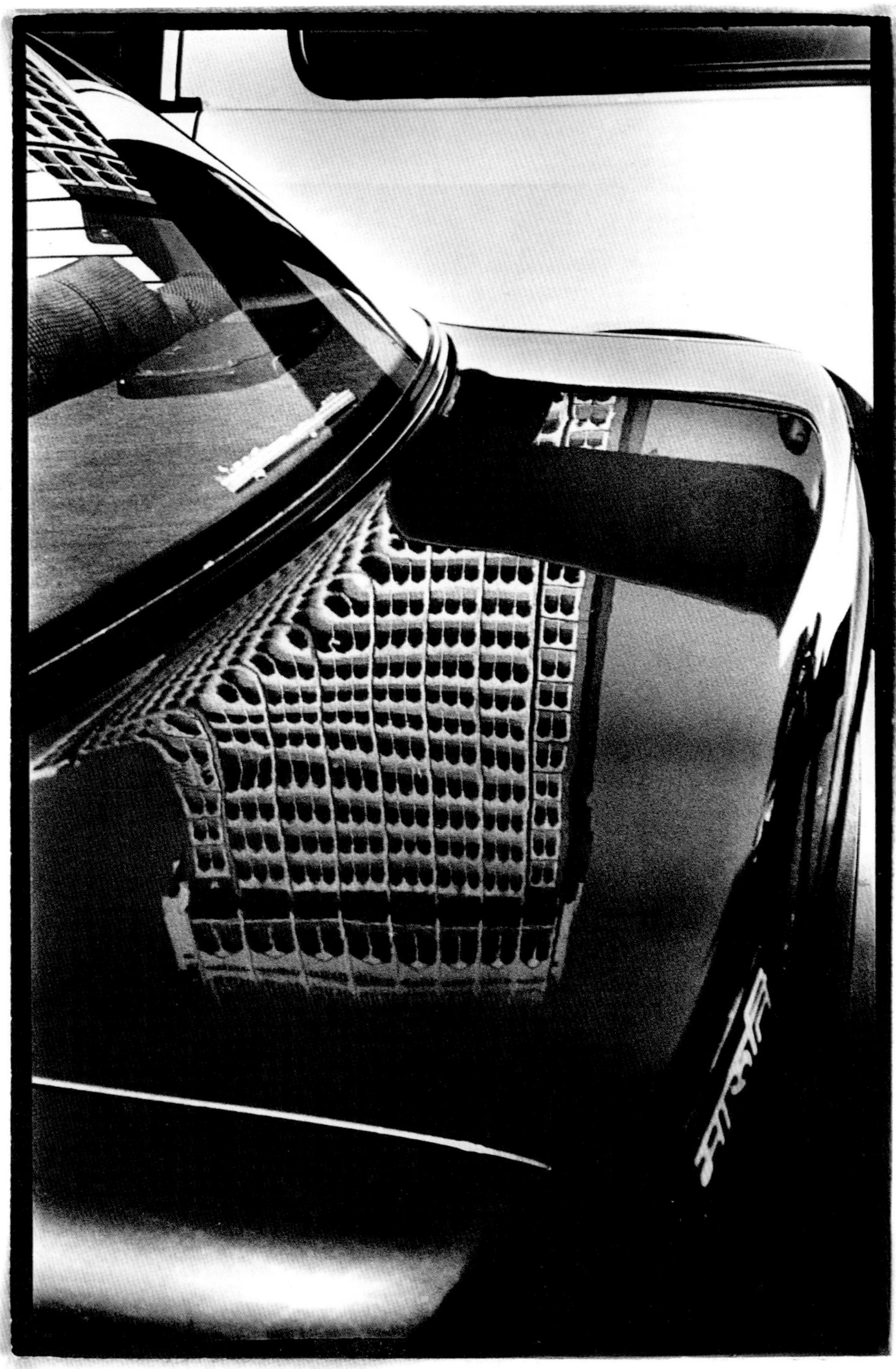

Vinit Chauhan
Taj Intercontinental Hotel, Apollo Bunder.

You do not have to open a door or peep through

a window to see life in Mumbai.

The walls are peeled away—the beautiful mosaic

is laid out for everyone to see.

Life happens not within walls, but outside them.

Anitha Balachandran

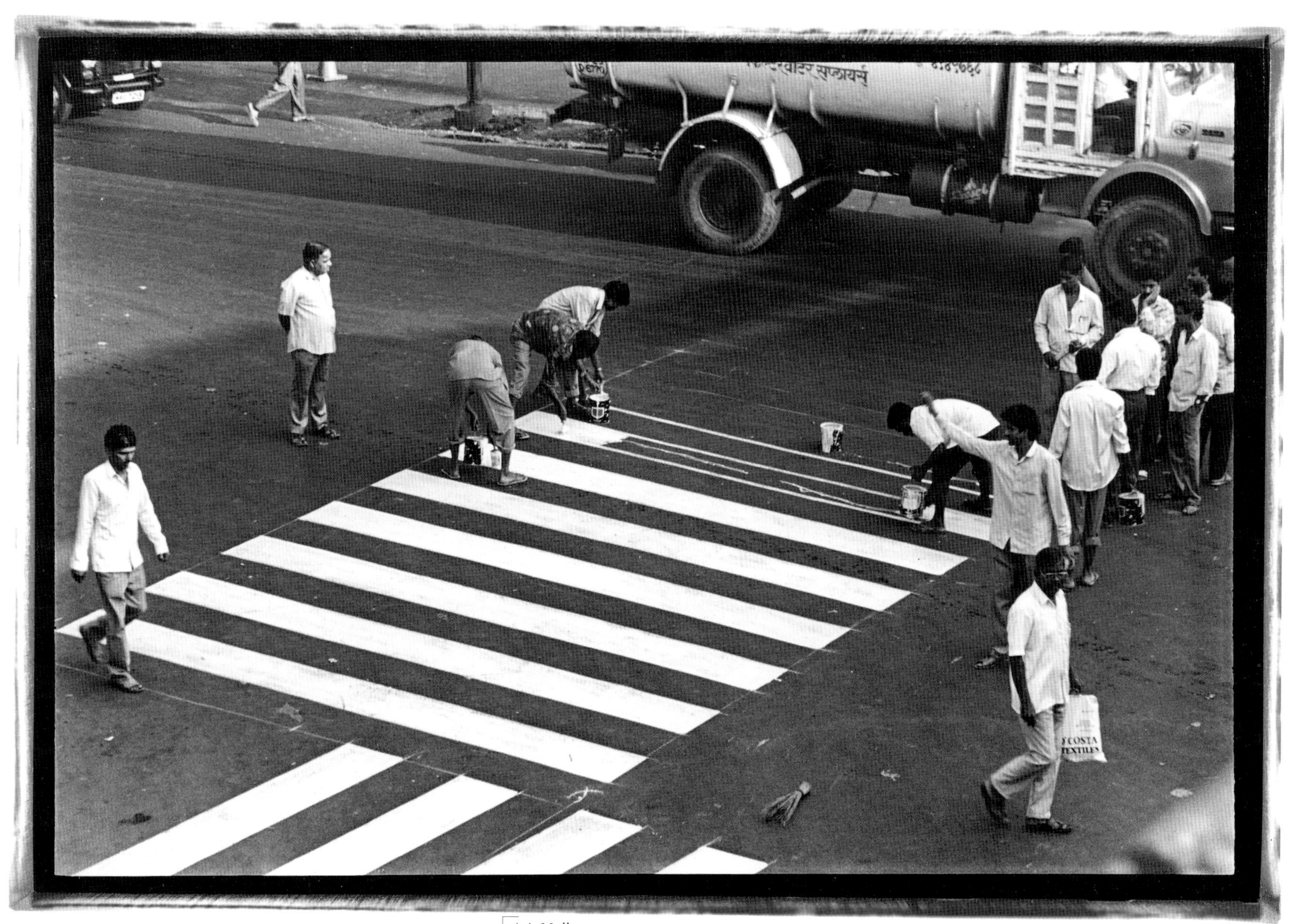

Asir Mulla
Lalbaug Fly-over, Dr. Ambedkar Road.

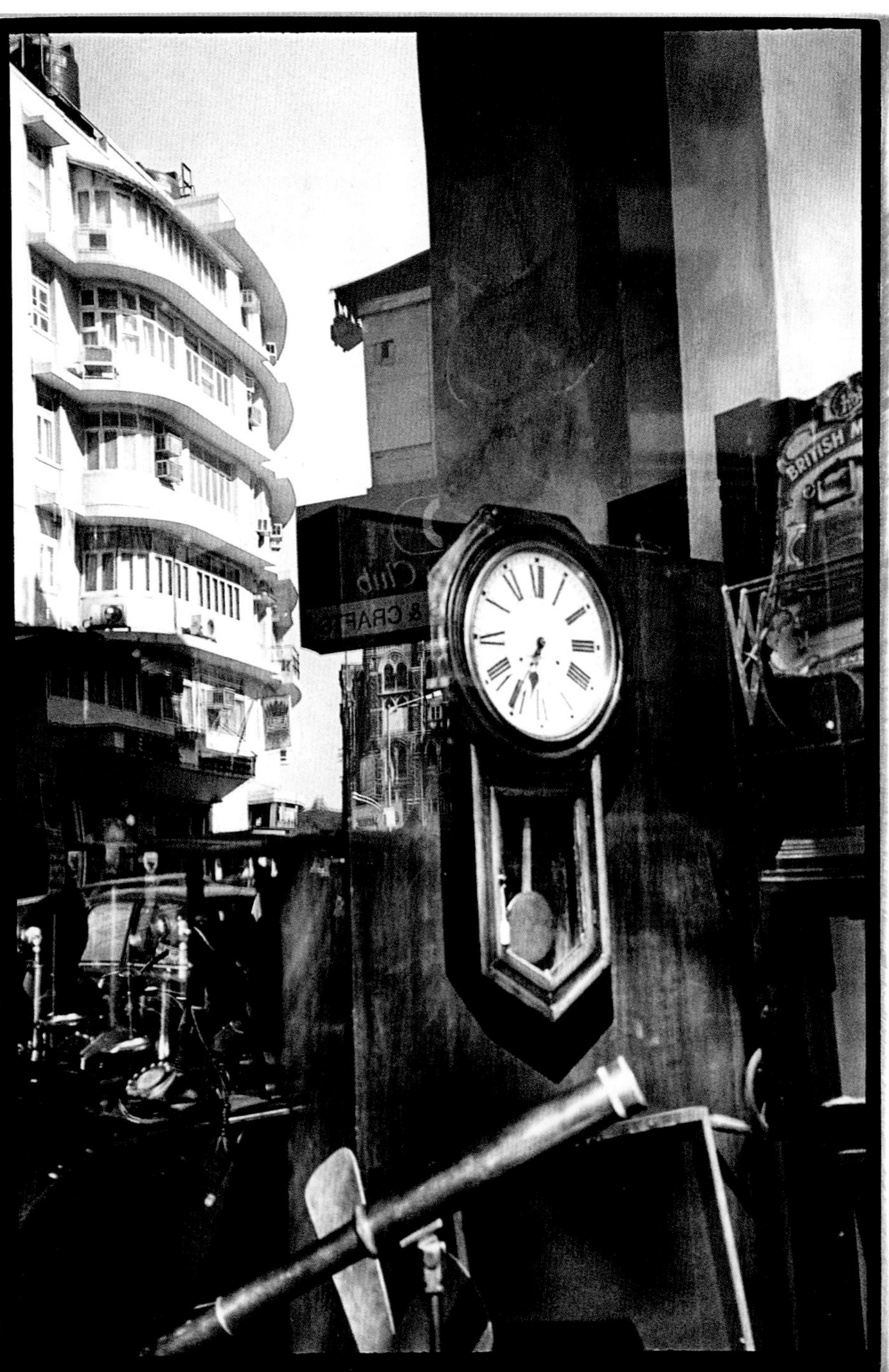

Nicole D'Souza
Near Regal Cinema, Landsdown Road, Colaba.

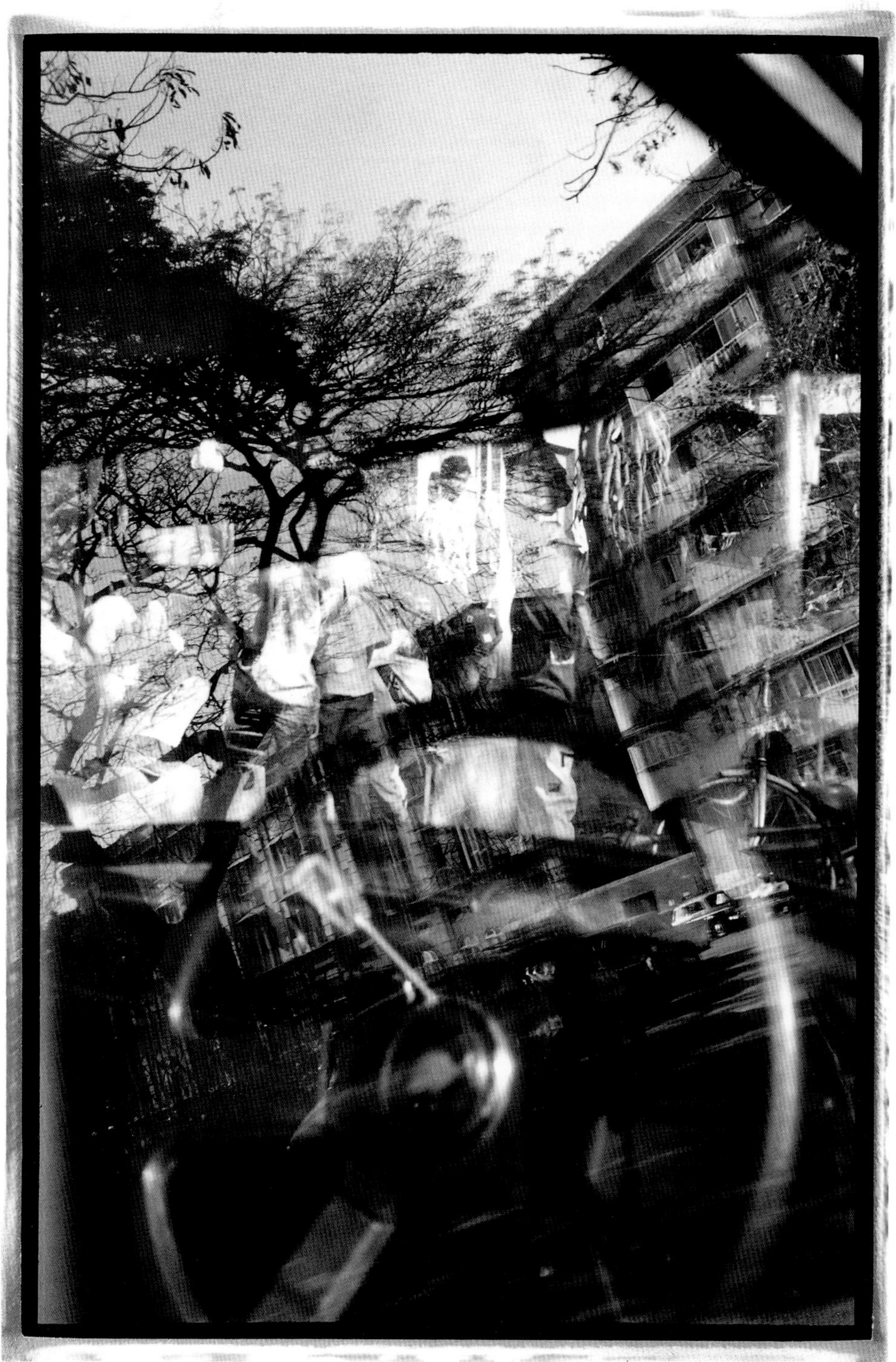

Vinit Chauhan
Mumbai Samachar Marg, Fort.

Sachin Sawant
Chatrapati Shivaji Terminus
(Victoria Terminus), Dadabhai Navroji Road.

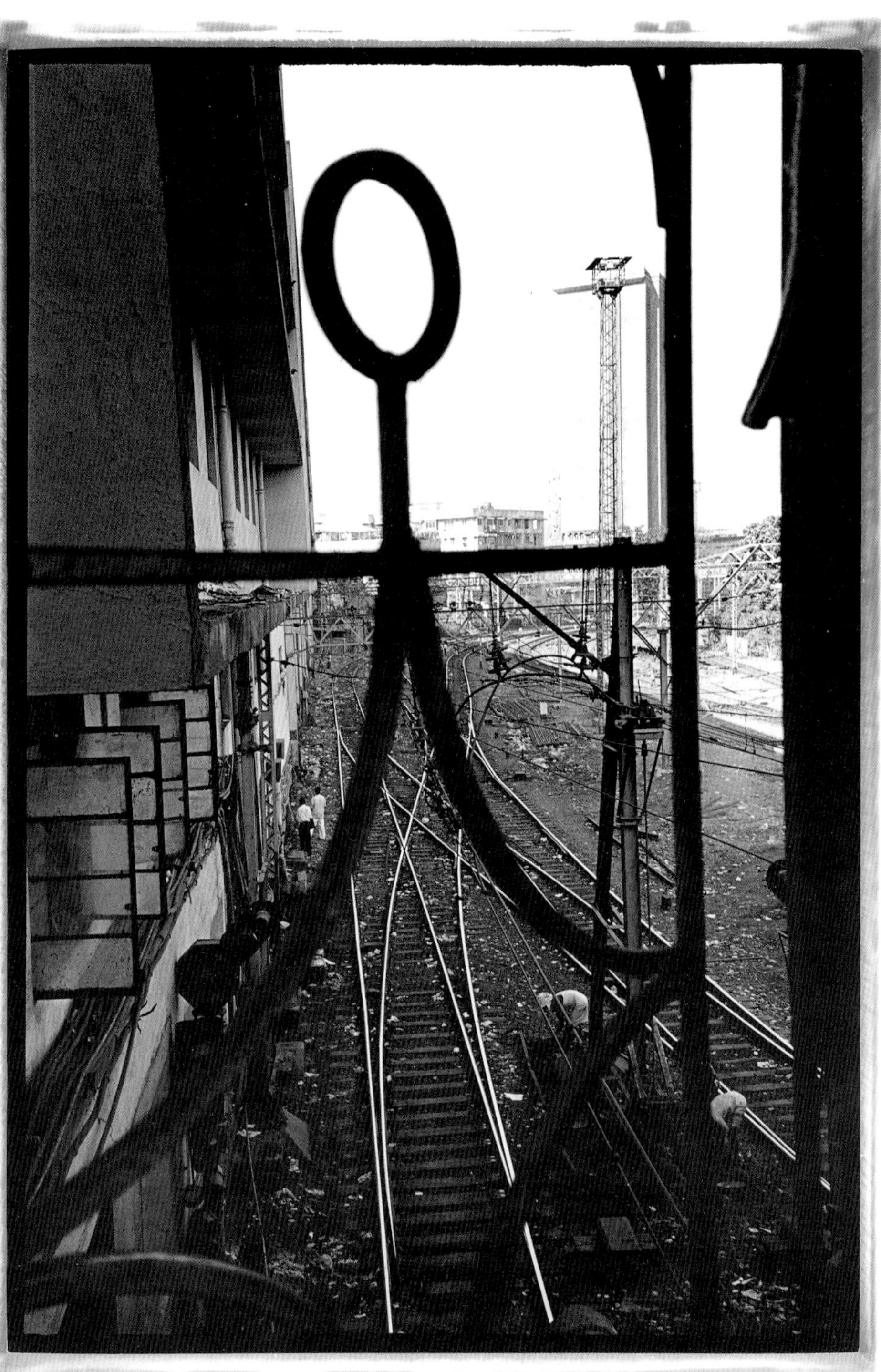

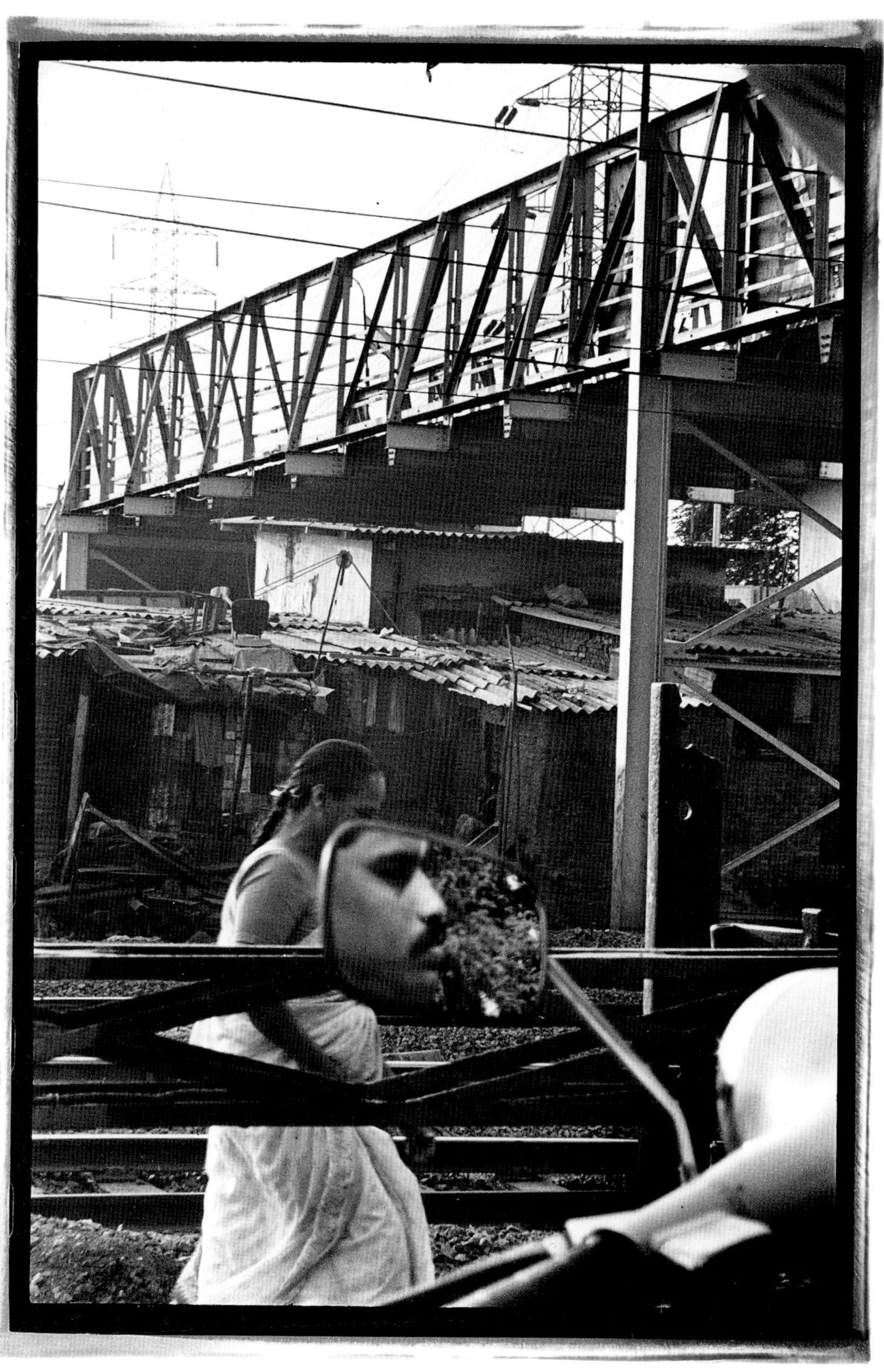

Vinit Chauhan
Bhandup Level Crossing, Bhandup.

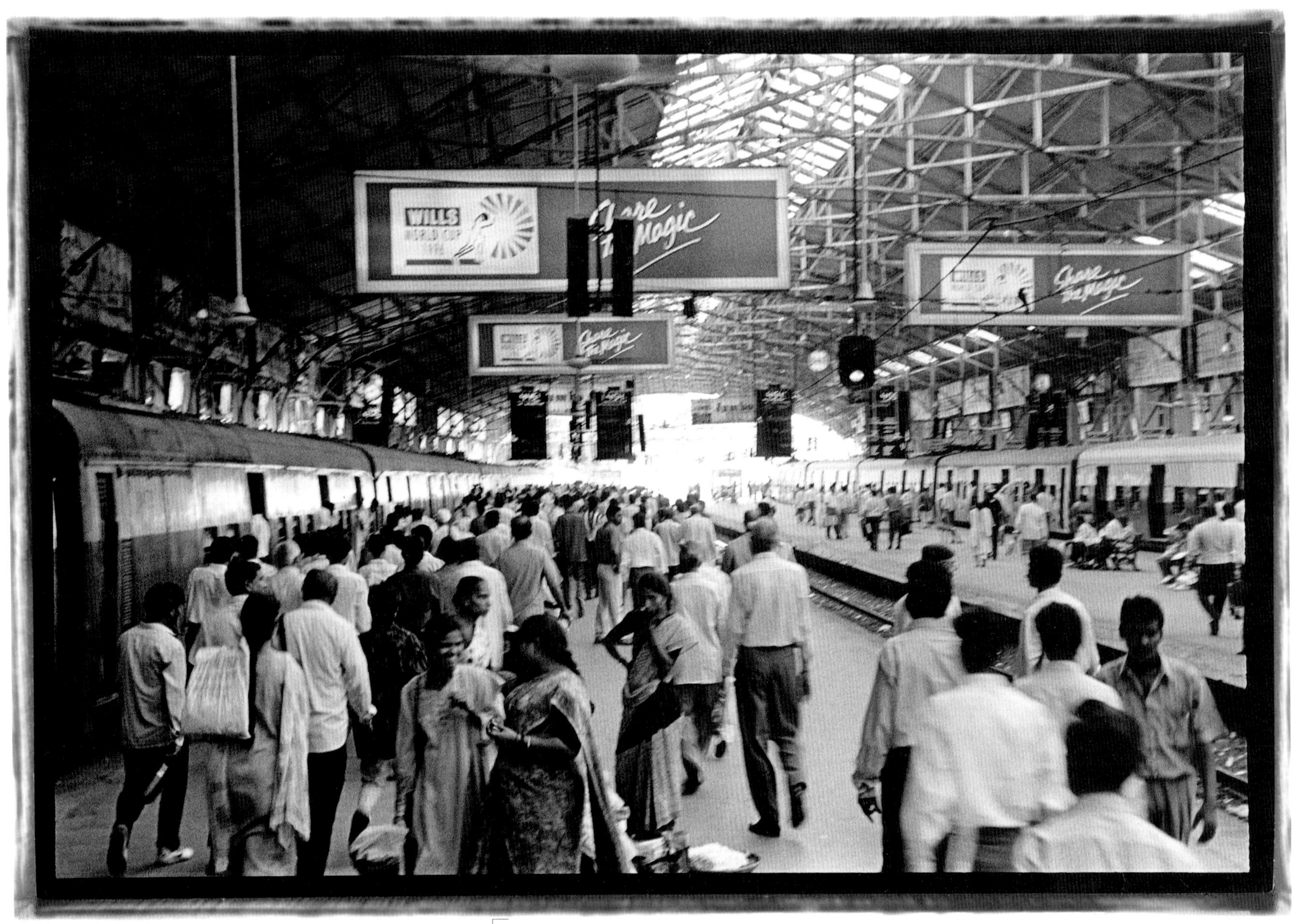

Yamini Hule
Churchgate Station, Veer Nariman Road.

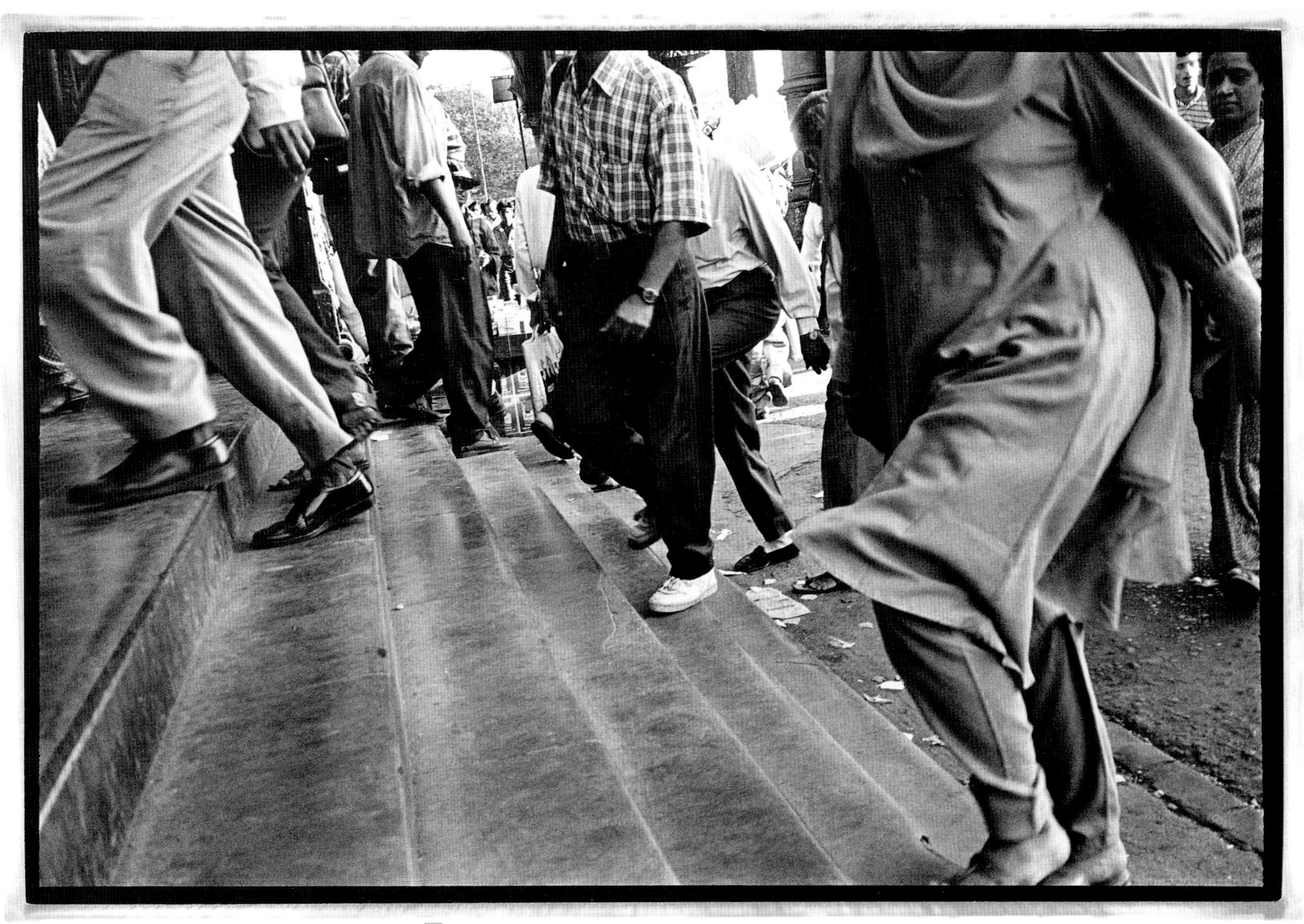

Asir Mulla
Chatrapati Shivaji Terminus (Victoria Terminus),
Dadabhai Navroji Road.

मेरा खेल का मैदान मेरे लिए अहम है। सब बच्चों के साथ वक्त गुज़ारना मुझे अच्छा लगता है। और मैं चाहता हूँ कि मैं हमेशा उनके साथ रहूँ।

मेरे साथी, कुनाल, विनोद, भुषण, समीर, संदीप और सचिन के साथ

भांडुप की खाड़ी में बैठकर पानी उछाँलने का मज़ा कुछ और ही है।

पाठशाला के ऑफ़ पीरियड में दोस्तों के साथ हँसी-मज़ाक करने में बड़ा मजा आता है। जी चाहता है कि ऐसे मौके बार बार मिलें।

मुझे मुंबई के गेटवे ऑफ़ इंडिया और एसेल वर्ल्ड बहुत अच्छे लगते हैं।

गरीब लोग भी दादर चौपाटी, जुहू, और हाजी अली में अपना दिल बहलाते हैं।

मेरे खयाल से अच्छे जीवन की खोज़ में मुंबई में आनेवाला हर देहाती भी वैशिष्ट्यपूर्ण है।

असीर मुल्ला

Translation in English on the facing page.

My playground is my landmark. I enjoy spending time with all the other children. I wish I could always be with them.

I love going to Bhandup Creek with my friends, Kunal, Vinod, Bhushan, Sameer, Sandeep, and Sachin splashing water with my feet while sitting by the creek.

I enjoy most the off periods I get in my school. That's when my friends and I get into a lot of mischief. I wish we could always have off periods. And, well, along with all these things I love the Gateway of India and Esselworld in Mumbai. Even the poor can entertain themselves at Dadar Chowpatti, Juhu, and Haji Ali.

I think that the people who come from the villages seeking a better life in Mumbai are also a landmark.

Asir Mulla

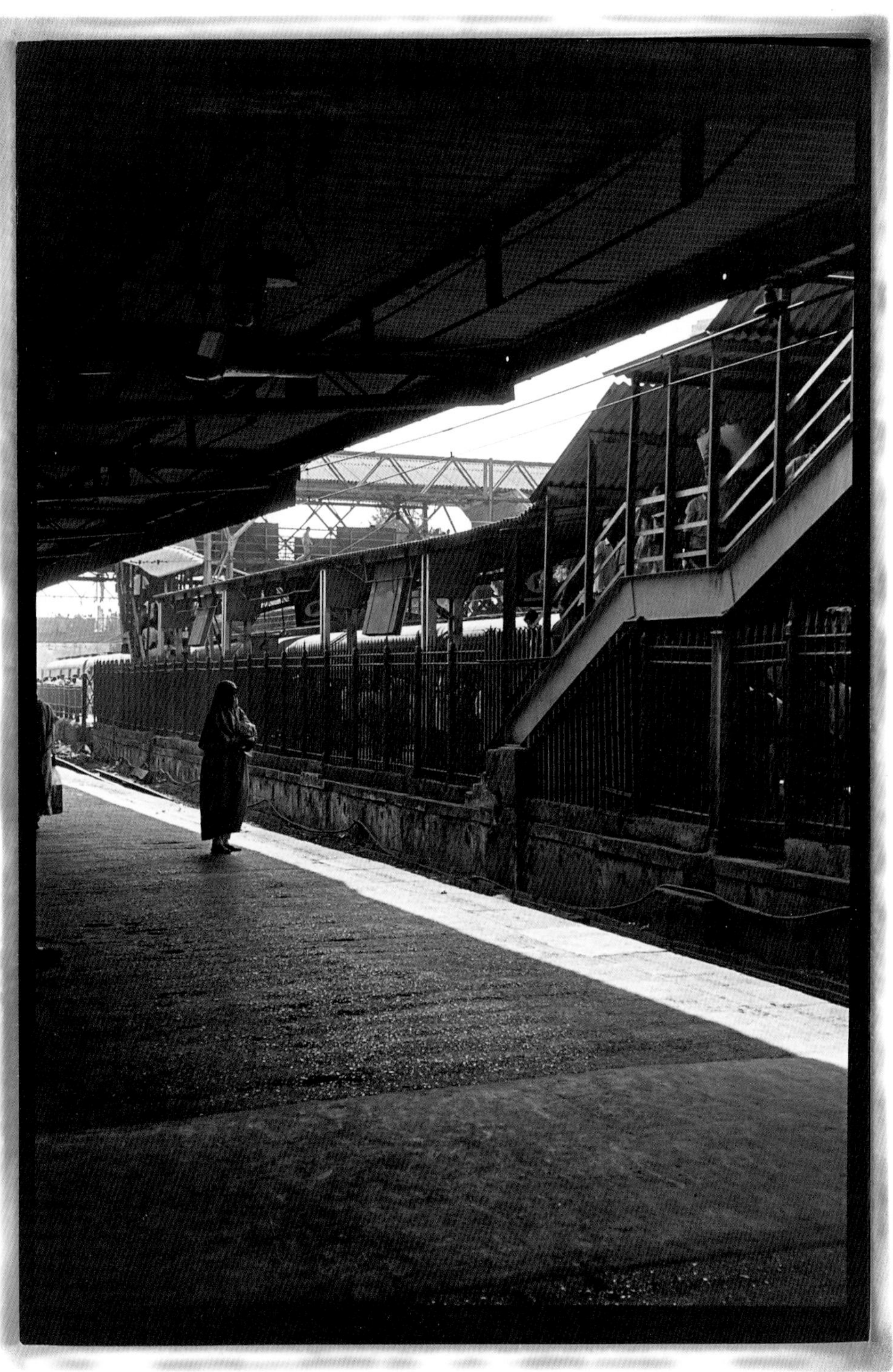

Nicole D'Souza
Dadar Station.

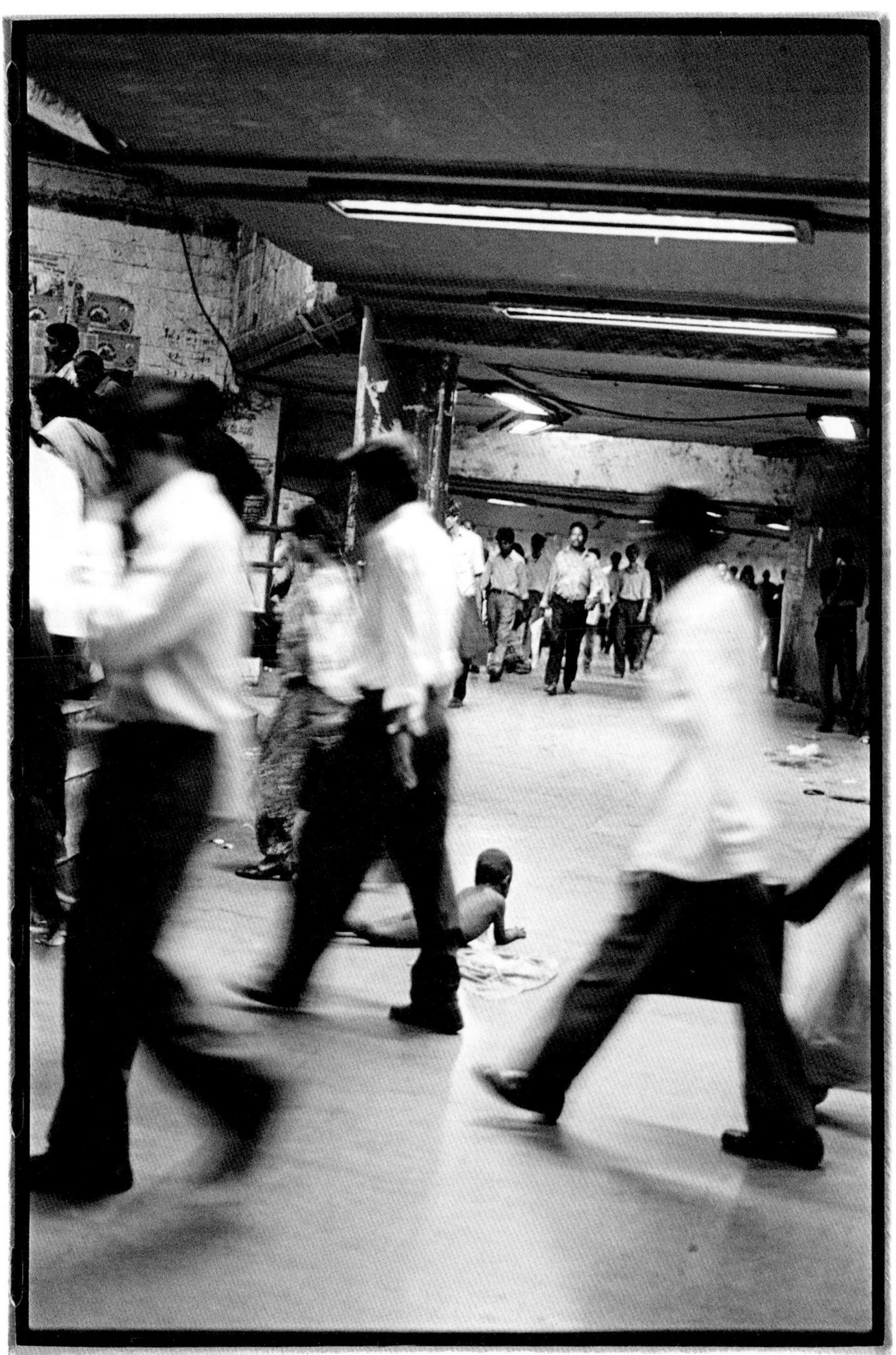

Bikram Mitra
Churchgate Subway, Veer Nariman Road.

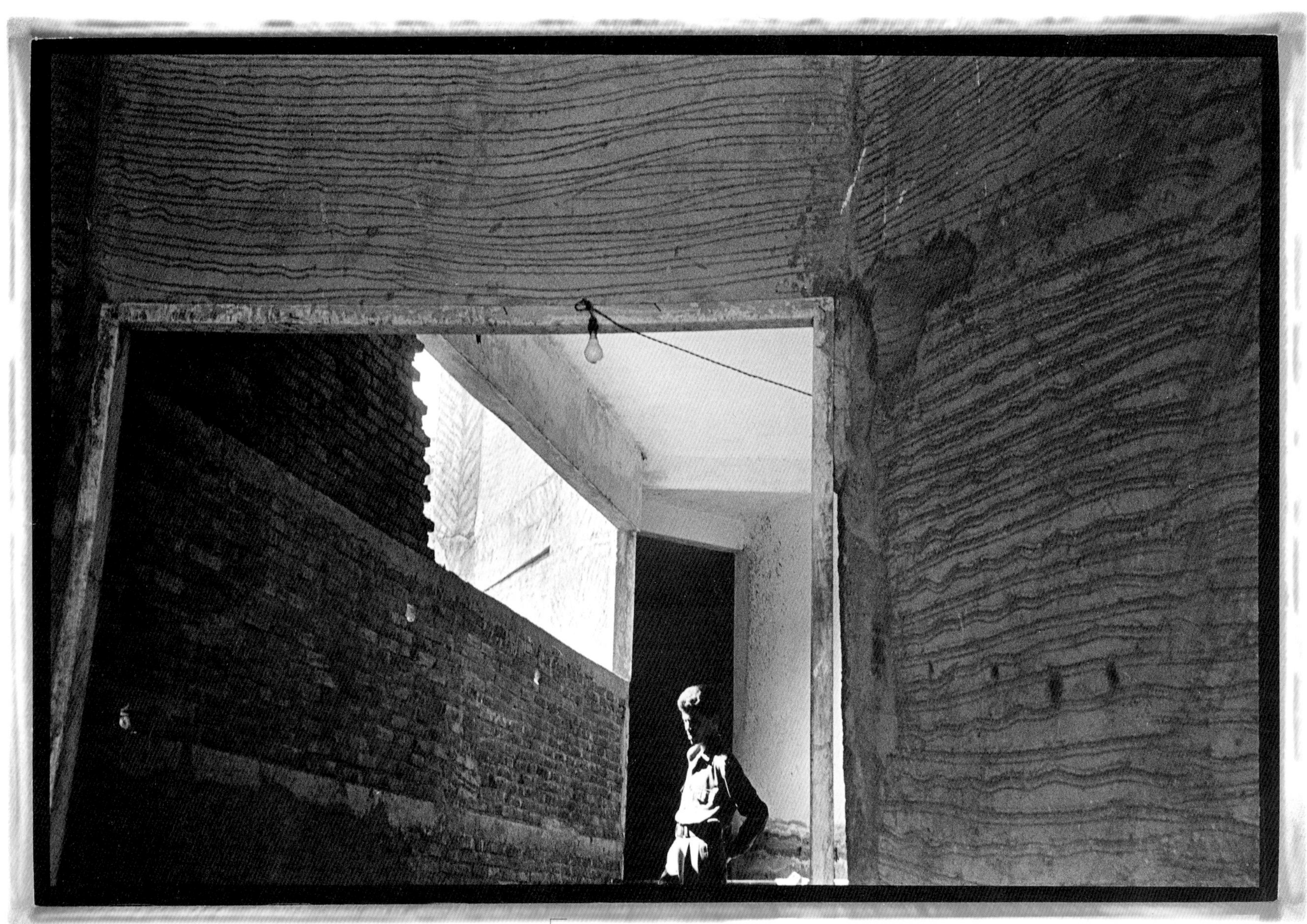

Vernon Fernandes
Pali Hill, Bandra.

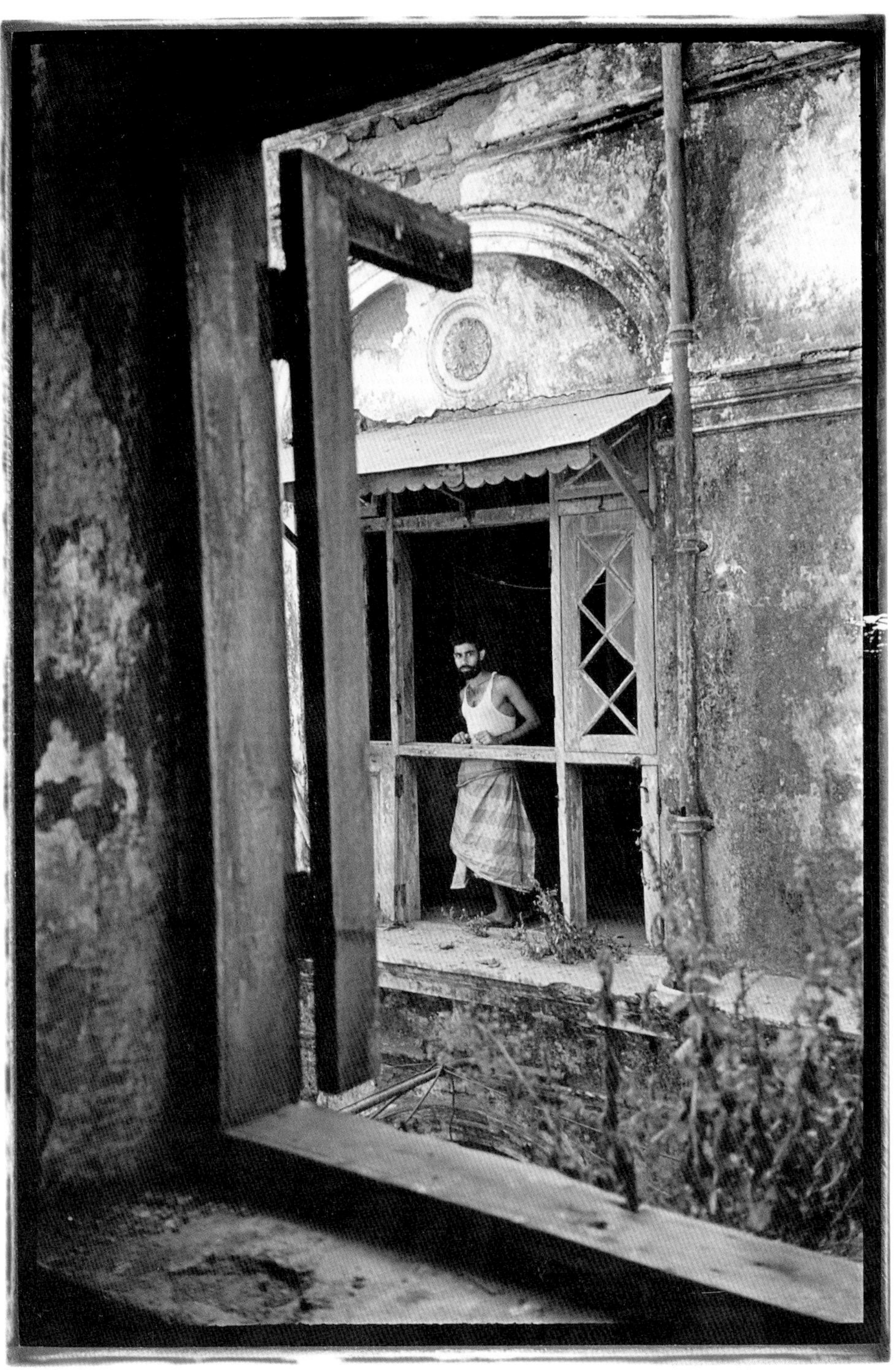

Nicole D'Souza
Charni Road, Girgaum.

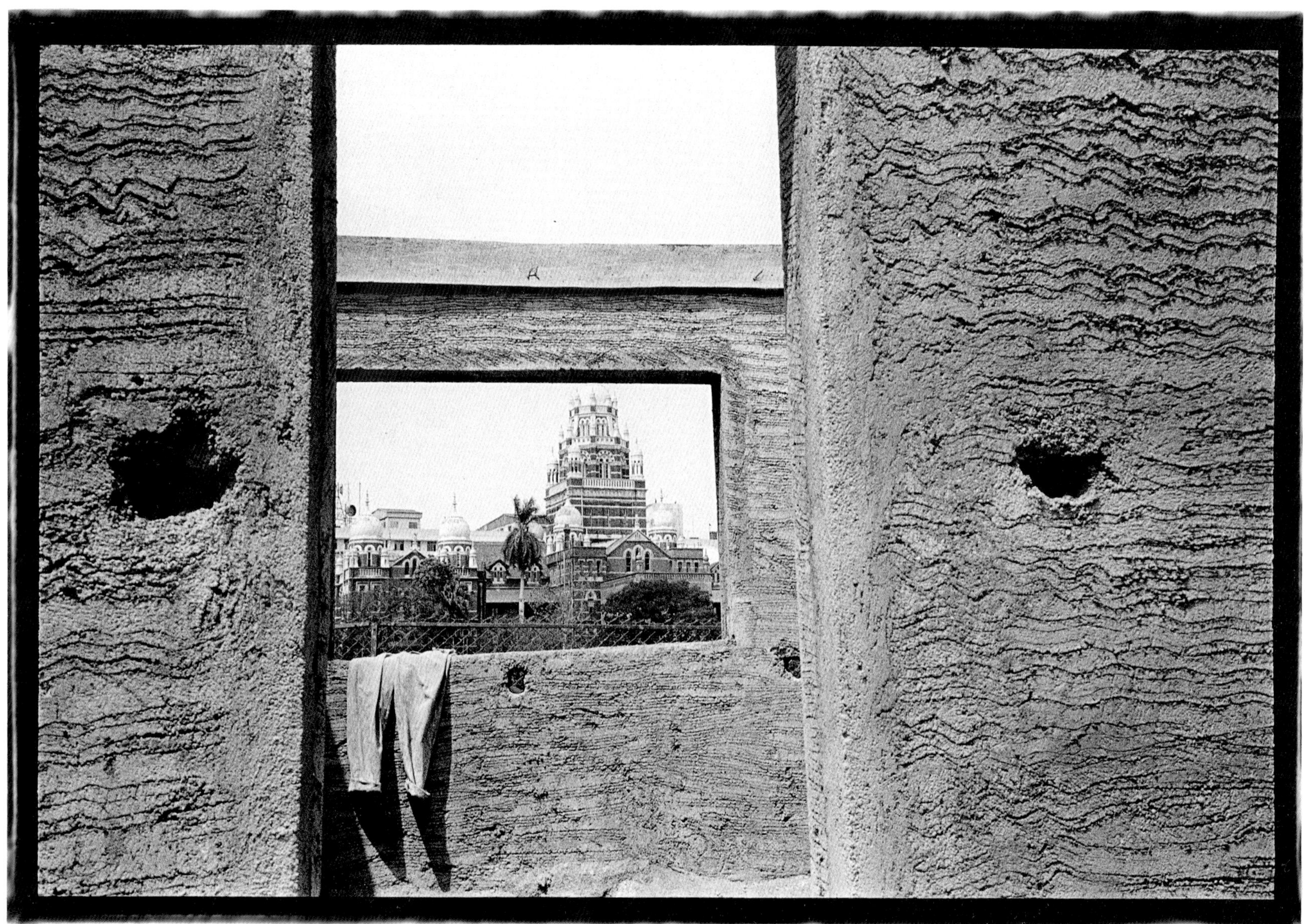

Anitha Balachandran
Western Railway Office, Veer Nariman Road, Churchgate.

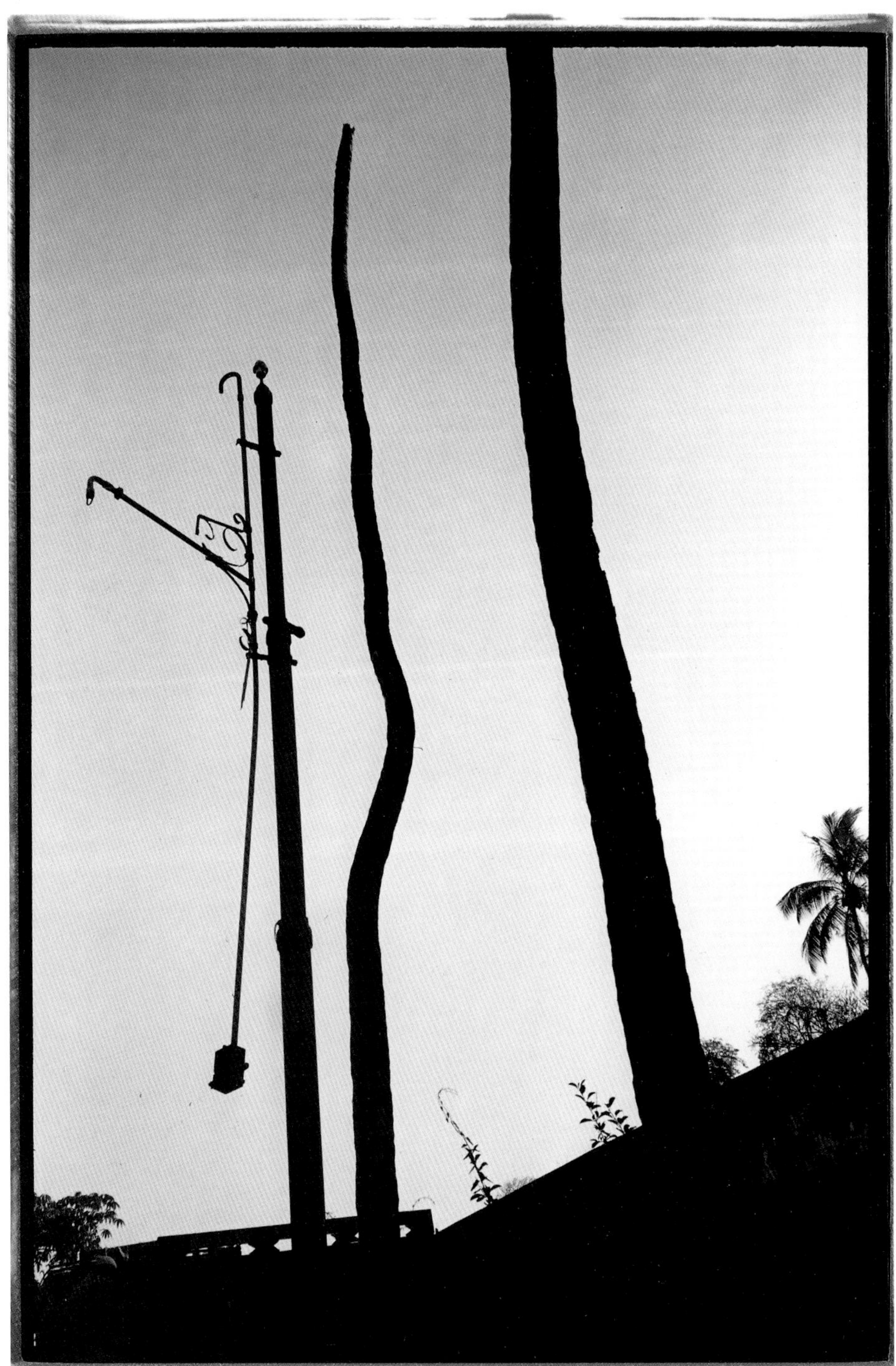

Nivedita Magar
Hyderabad Estate, Napean Sea Road.

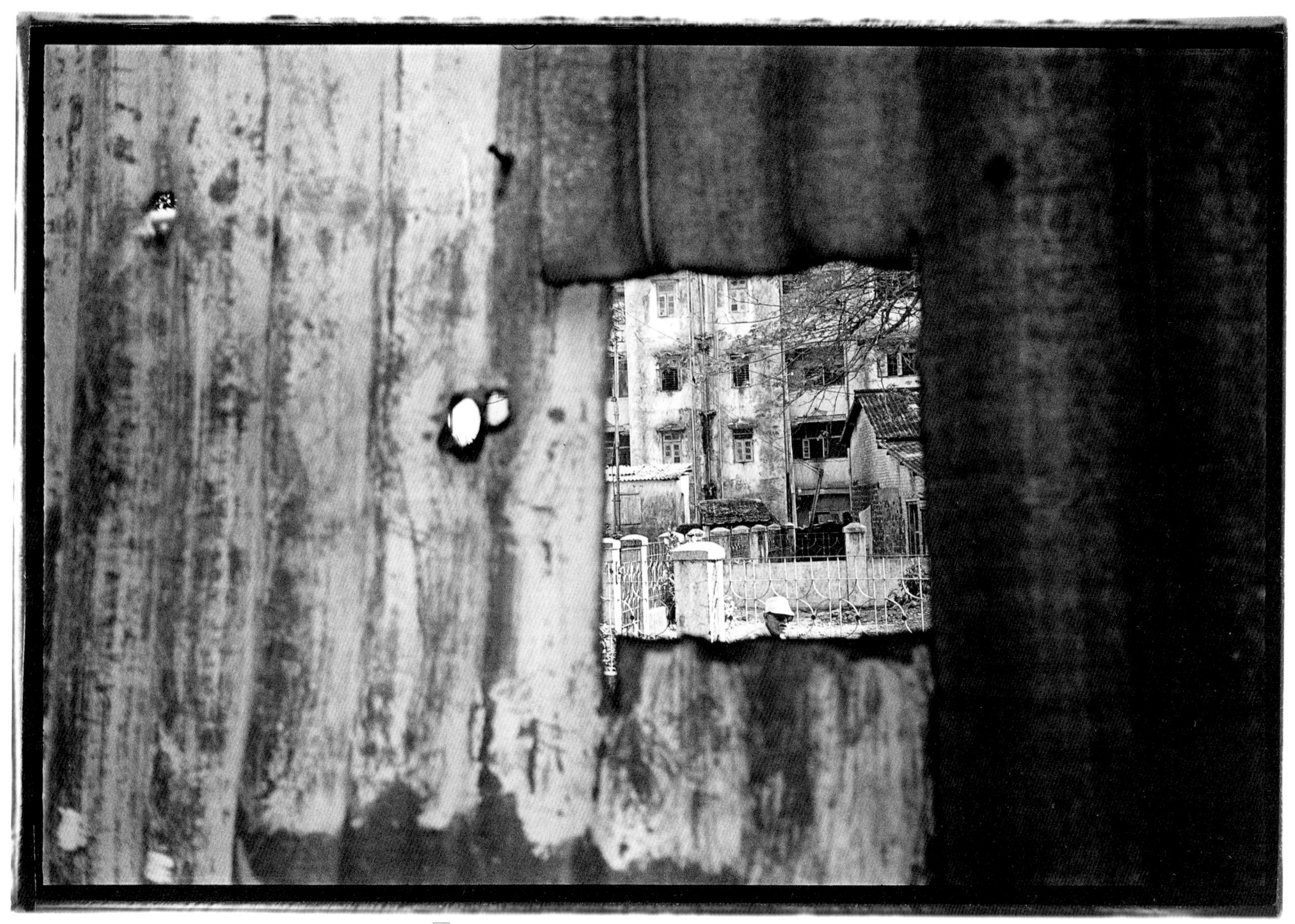

Nivedita Magar
Byculla Bridge, Balwantsingh Dhodi Marg, Mazagaon.

I think people are landmarks more than we imagine. The people we see, we speak to, bump into, or try to ignore. What would this city be to me without them? Just an empty shell.
A city is like a rough stone—you can't know it till you turn it around and see it and feel it from every angle. The young, the old, the rich, the poor—every texture has to be seen and felt.

Anitha Balachandran

Nicole D'Souza

Mahalaxmi Race Course,
Dr. E. Moses Road.

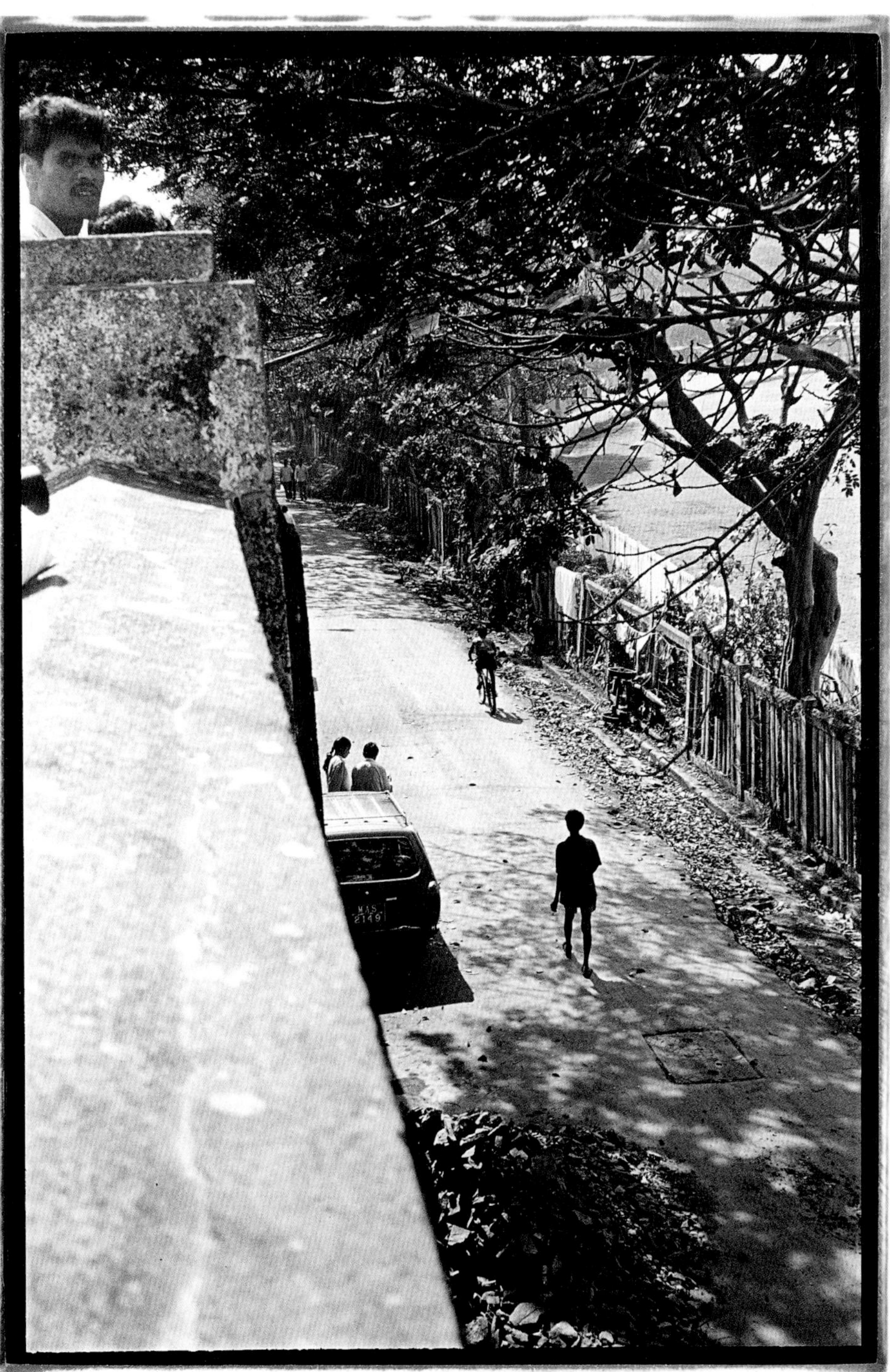

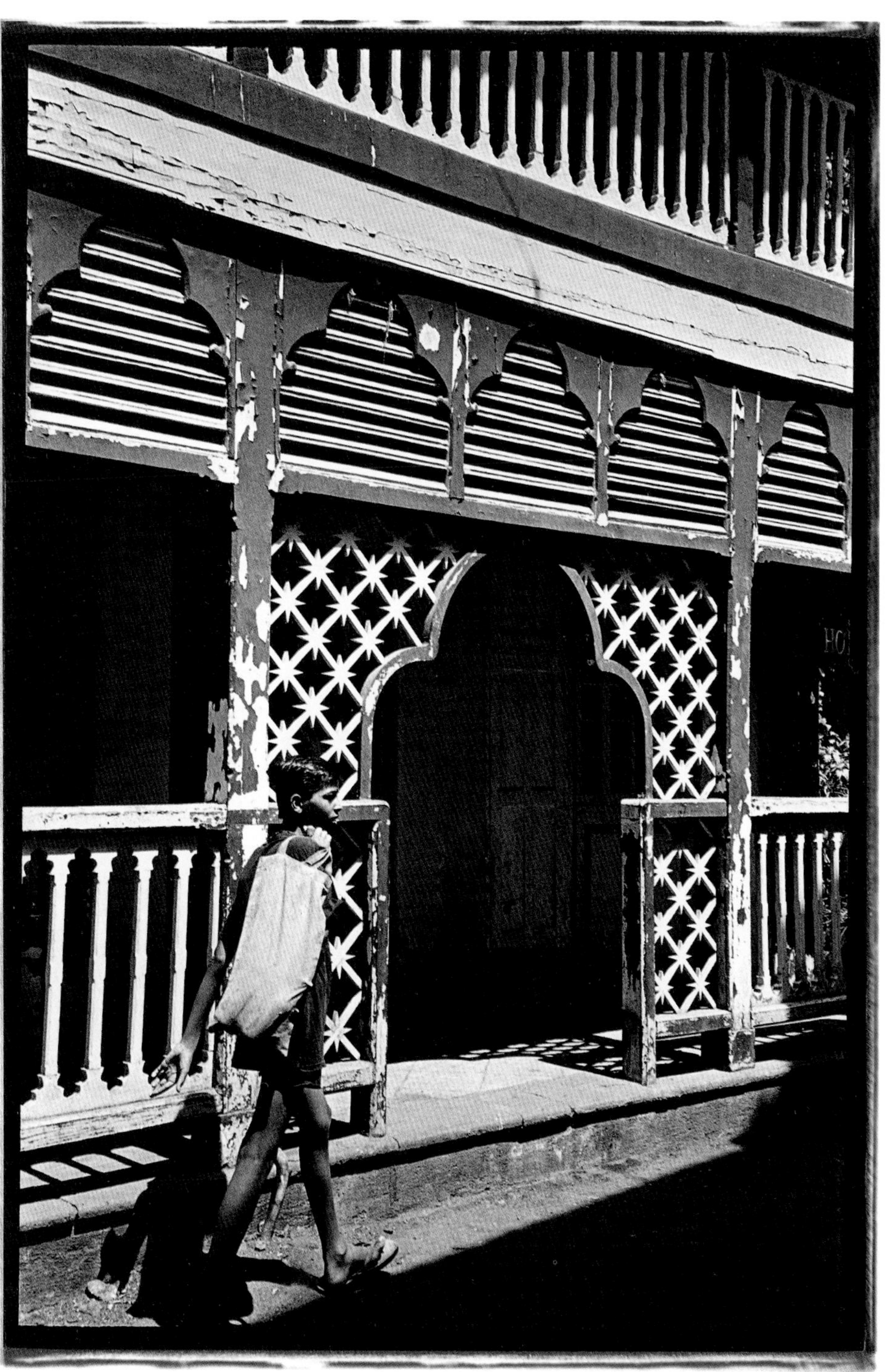

Anitha Balachandran
Khotachi Wadi,
near Anant Ashram, Girgaum.

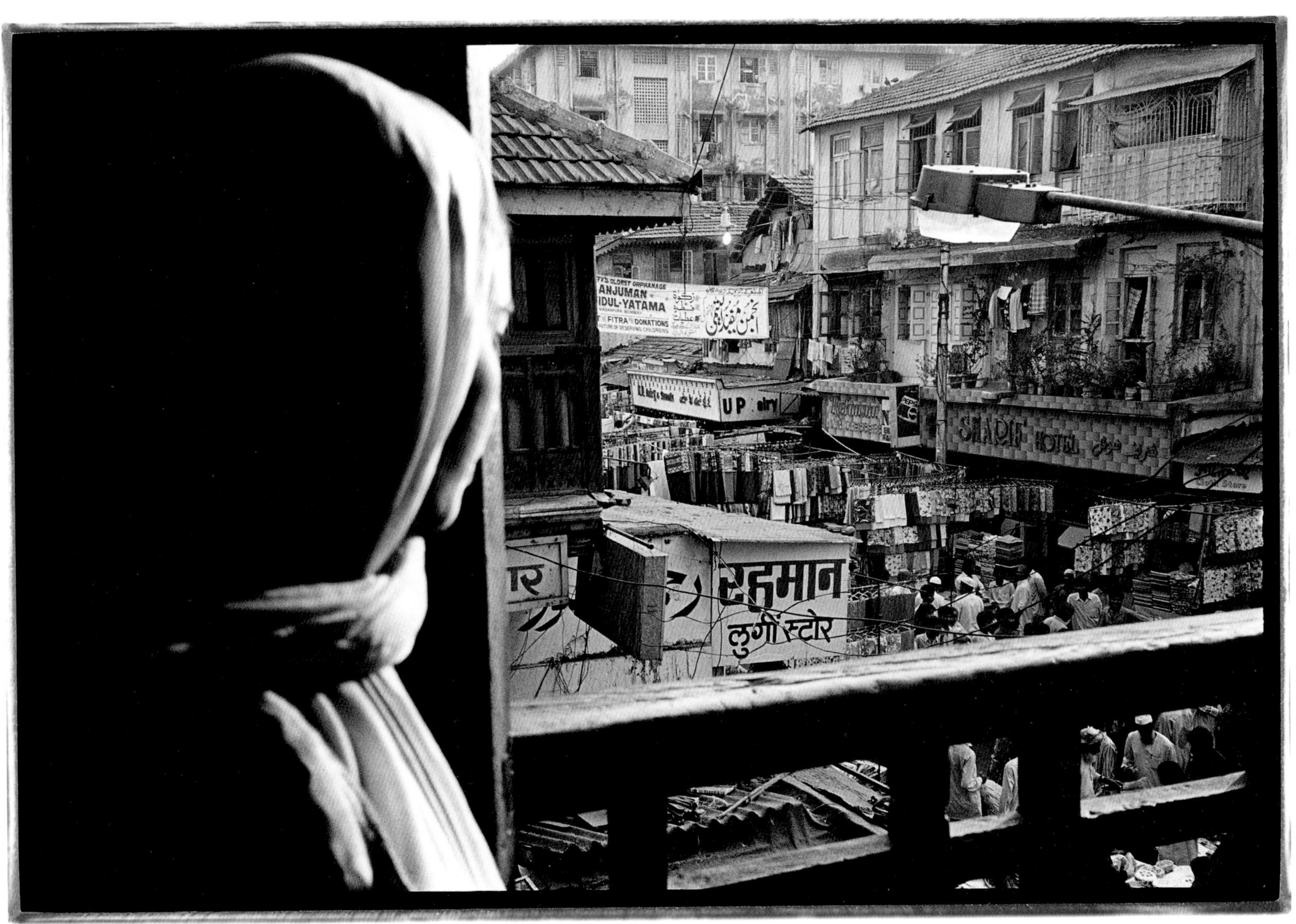

Nivedita Magar
Ramzan - Madanpura, off Mohammed Ali Road.

*If migratory birds restricted themselves to
native areas and didn't migrate, their life
would become difficult.
Similarly for culture to survive it is natural
to assimilate other influences.*

जसे पक्ष्यांनी स्थलांतर केले नाही तर त्यांचे जीवन मुश्कील होईल.

त्याचप्रमाणे संस्कृतीची देवाण-घेवाण हा जीवनाचा एक नैसर्गिक

भाग आहे.

Yamini Hule

*Old buildings store old stories.
If we break these buildings - the
stories are finished.*

Vinit Chauhan

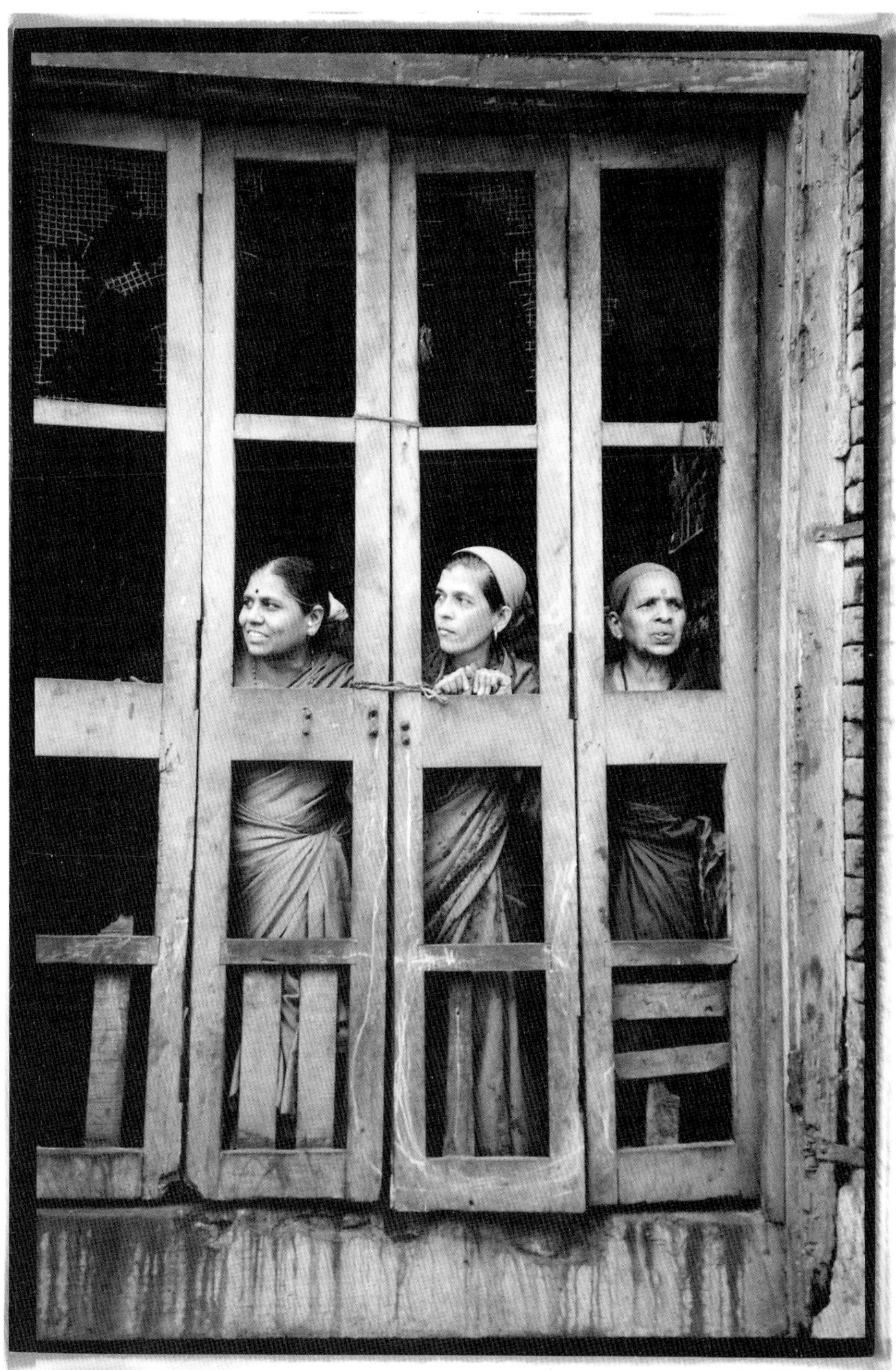

Yamini Hule
Industrial Estate, P. D'Mello Road, Masjid.

Yamini Hule
Iftar during Ramzan,
Mohammed Ali Road.

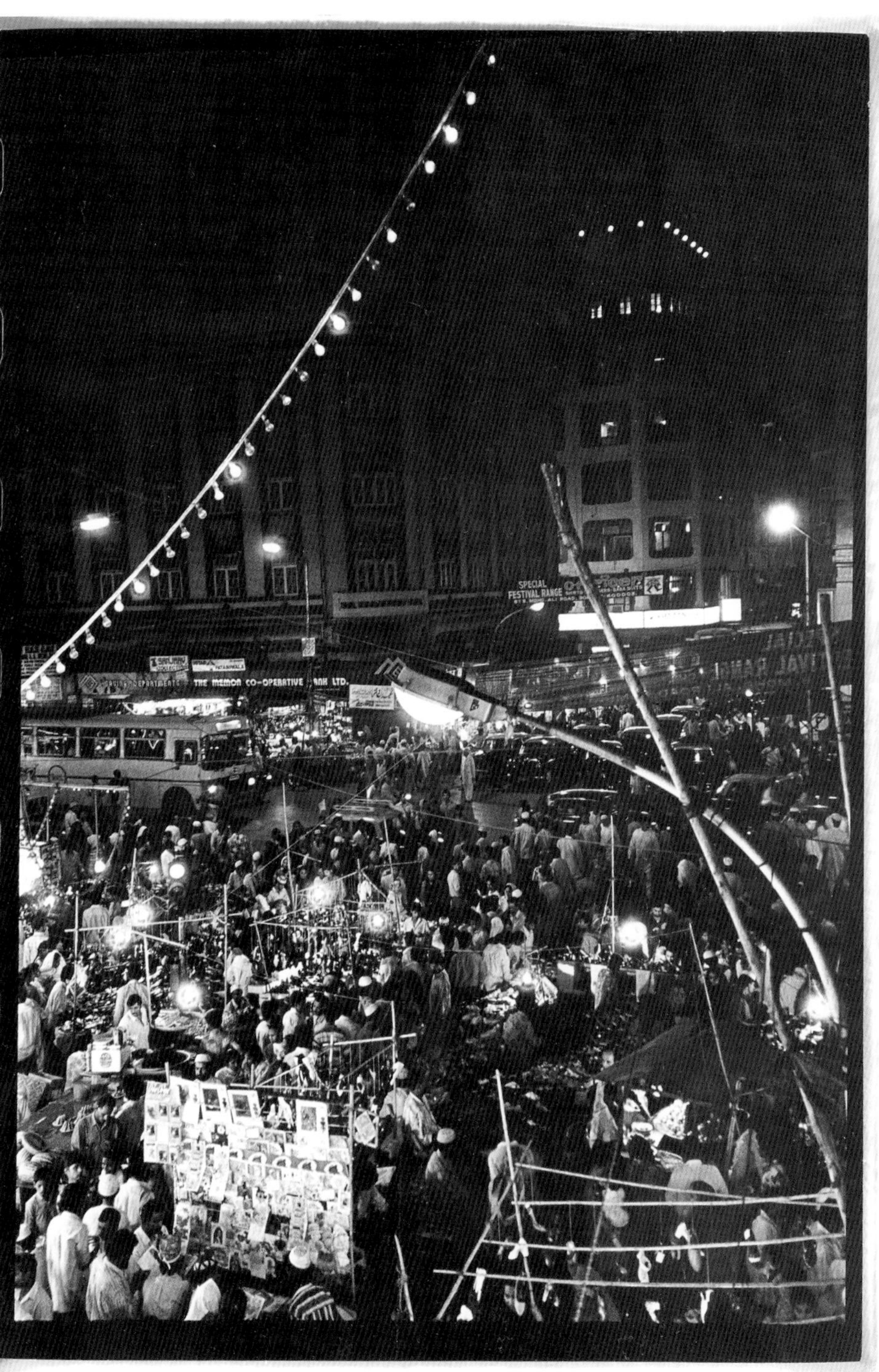

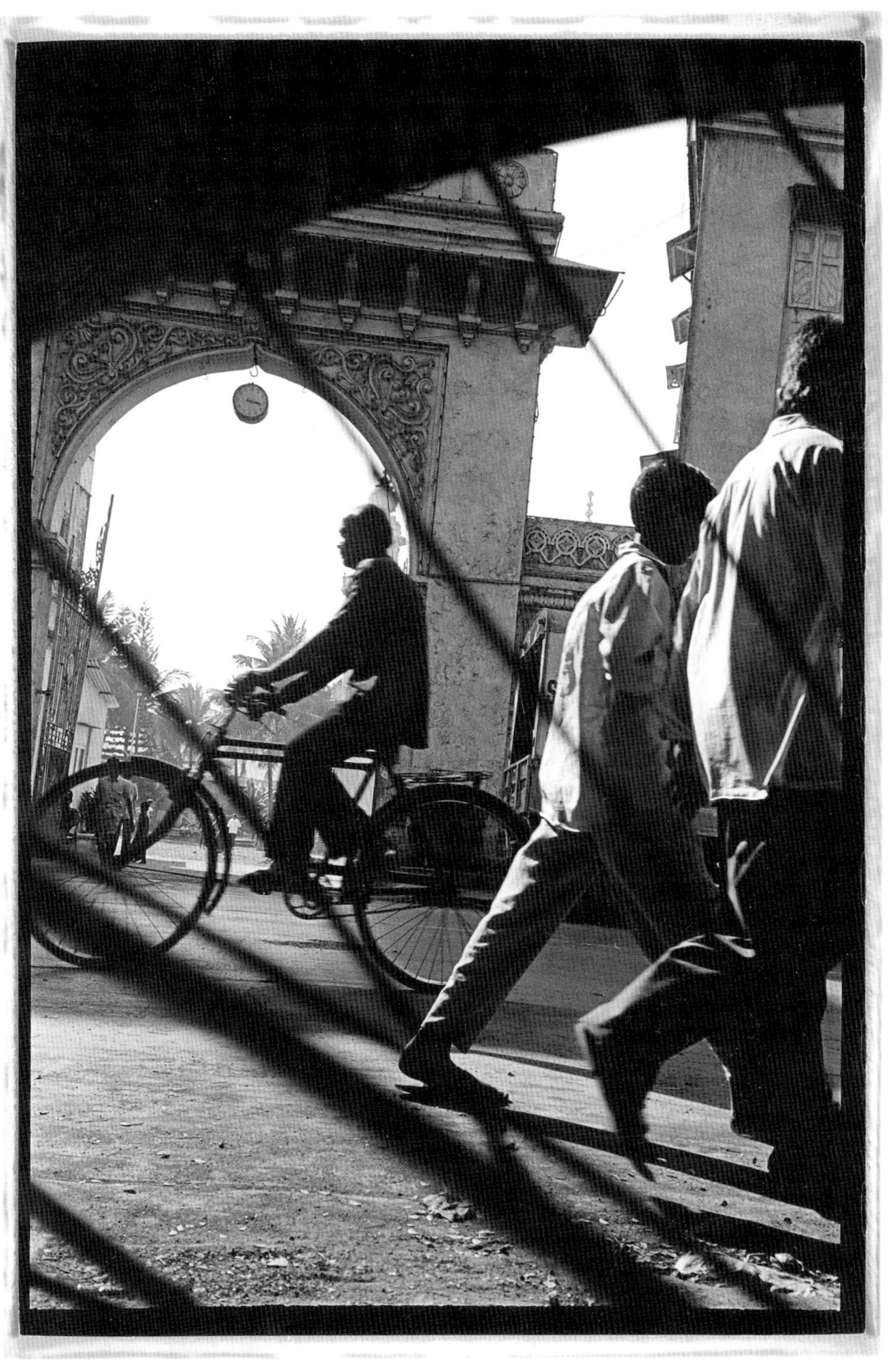

Sachin Sawant
Chor Bazaar, off Mohammed Ali Road.

A landmark tells me that I am not lost. Something I search for—or avoid.

The new is as much of a landmark as the old. Often it is the point at which they spill over into each other creating unique patterns and images that is a landmark.
Trees mark the land as much as the piles of stones and concrete that people put together. They seem to extend their branches like fingers trying to grasp the air and smells—the essence of a city.

Anitha Balachandran

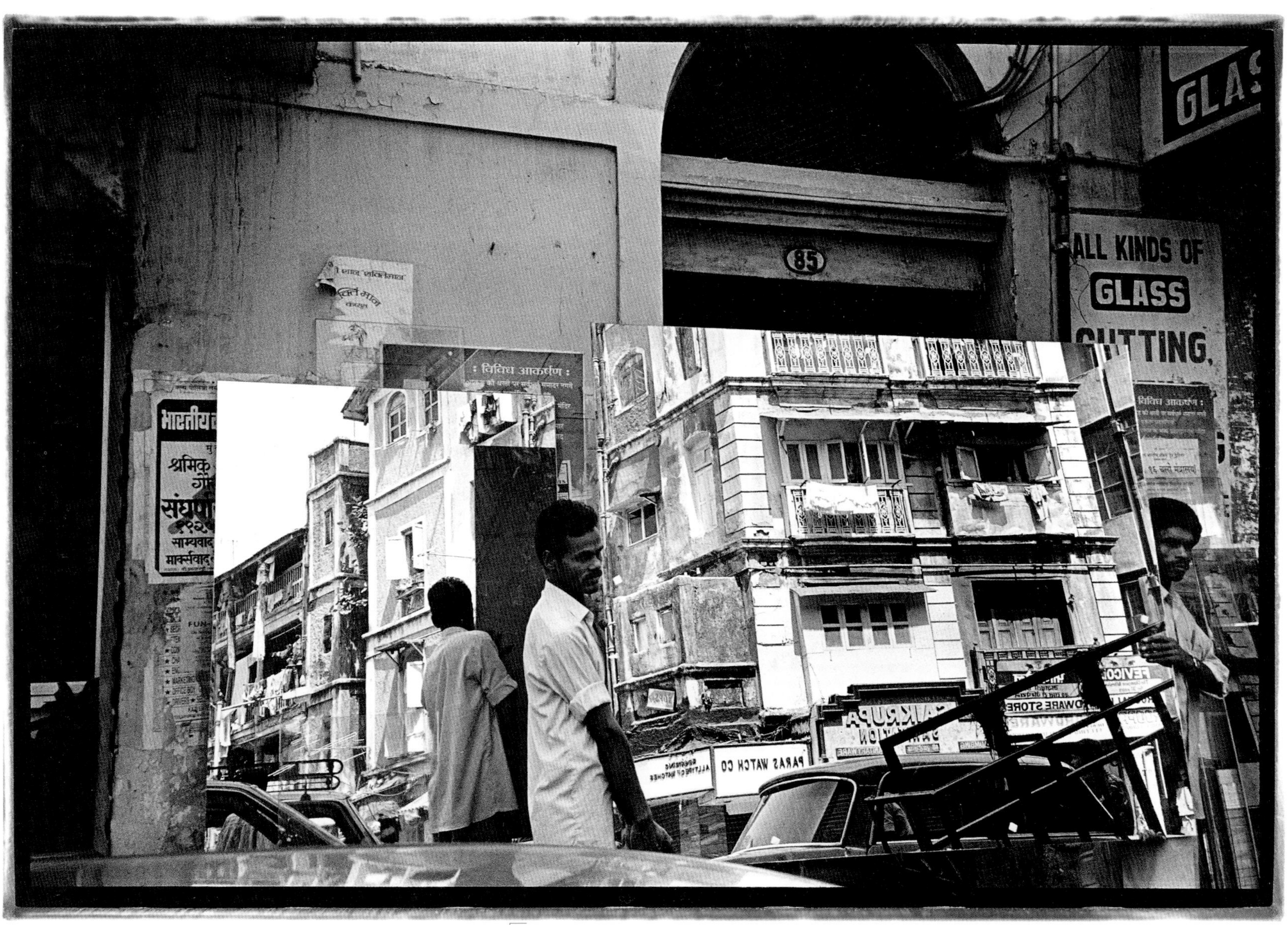

Nivedita Magar
Abdul Rehman Street, Pydhuni.

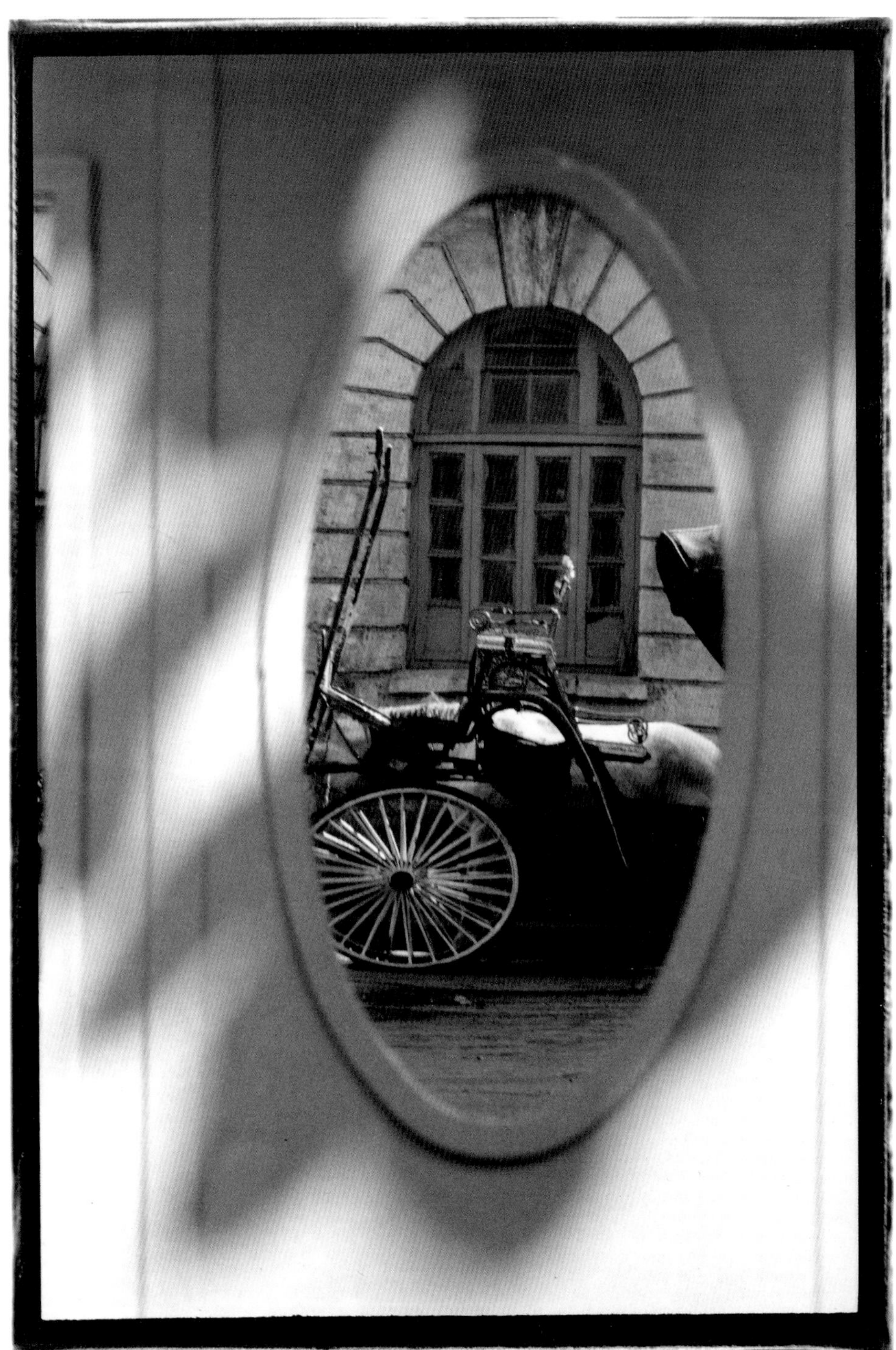

Yamini Hule

Cupboard Street Market,
Yusuf Meherali Road.

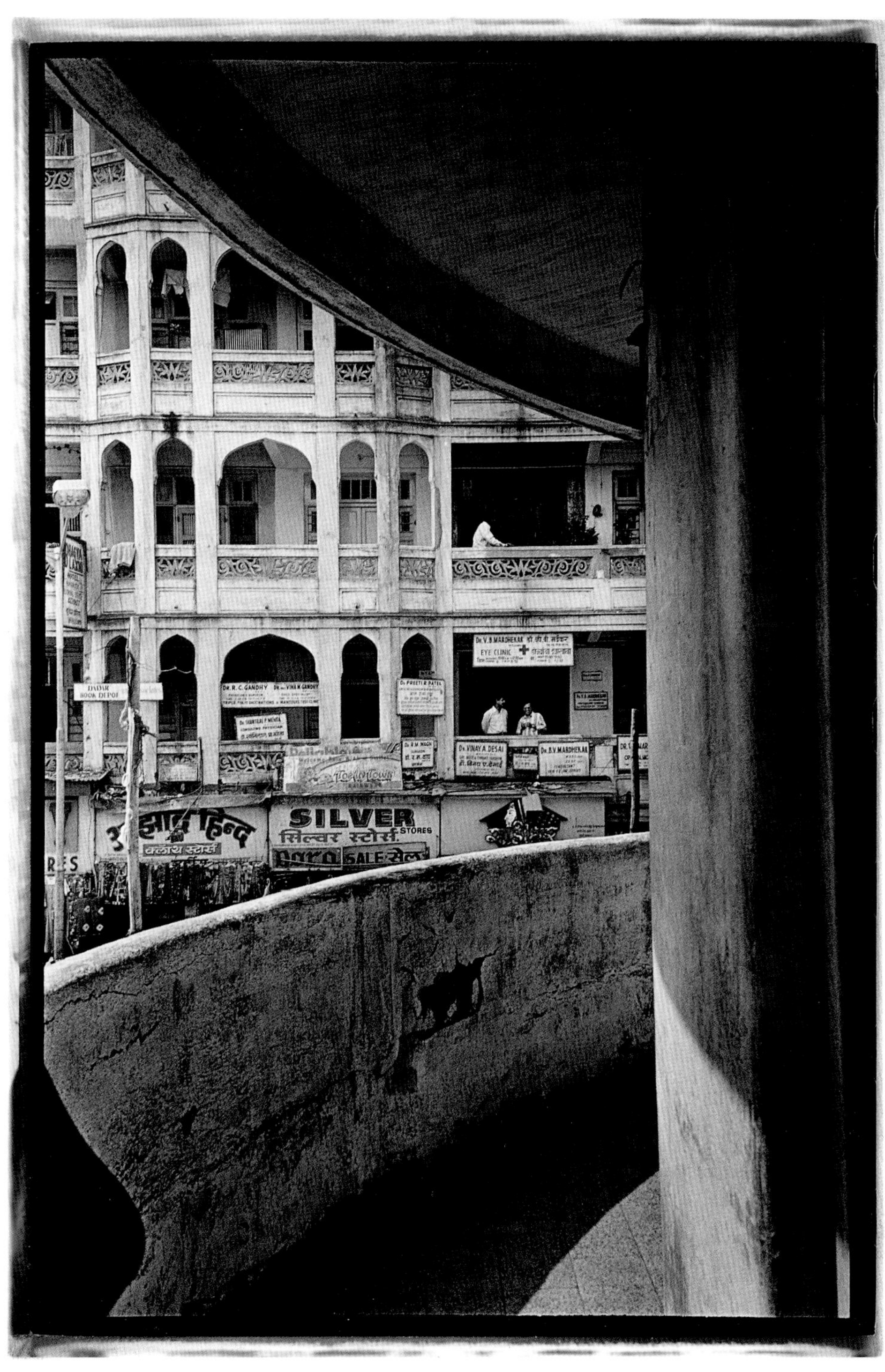

Sachin Sawant
Dadar Station, Senapati Bapat Marg.

Never been to all the parts of Bombay before. Working on the project showed me these areas.

It was fun just being with other children.

Mom would make me study on holidays but with the project I looked forward to getting out on the street, especially at night.

When travelling by train, I can't help thinking of all the picture frames passing by.

Normally most people feel the folk in their buildings are all they know, but I feel I know all of Bandra and I am part of it, even if it has changed into a city-like place.

When buildings go, like a beautiful bungalow down the street, I sometimes can't remember what it was like. That's why I'd like to photograph it.

Wish Bandra would not change at all and stay just the way it is.

⌐Vernon Fernandes⌐

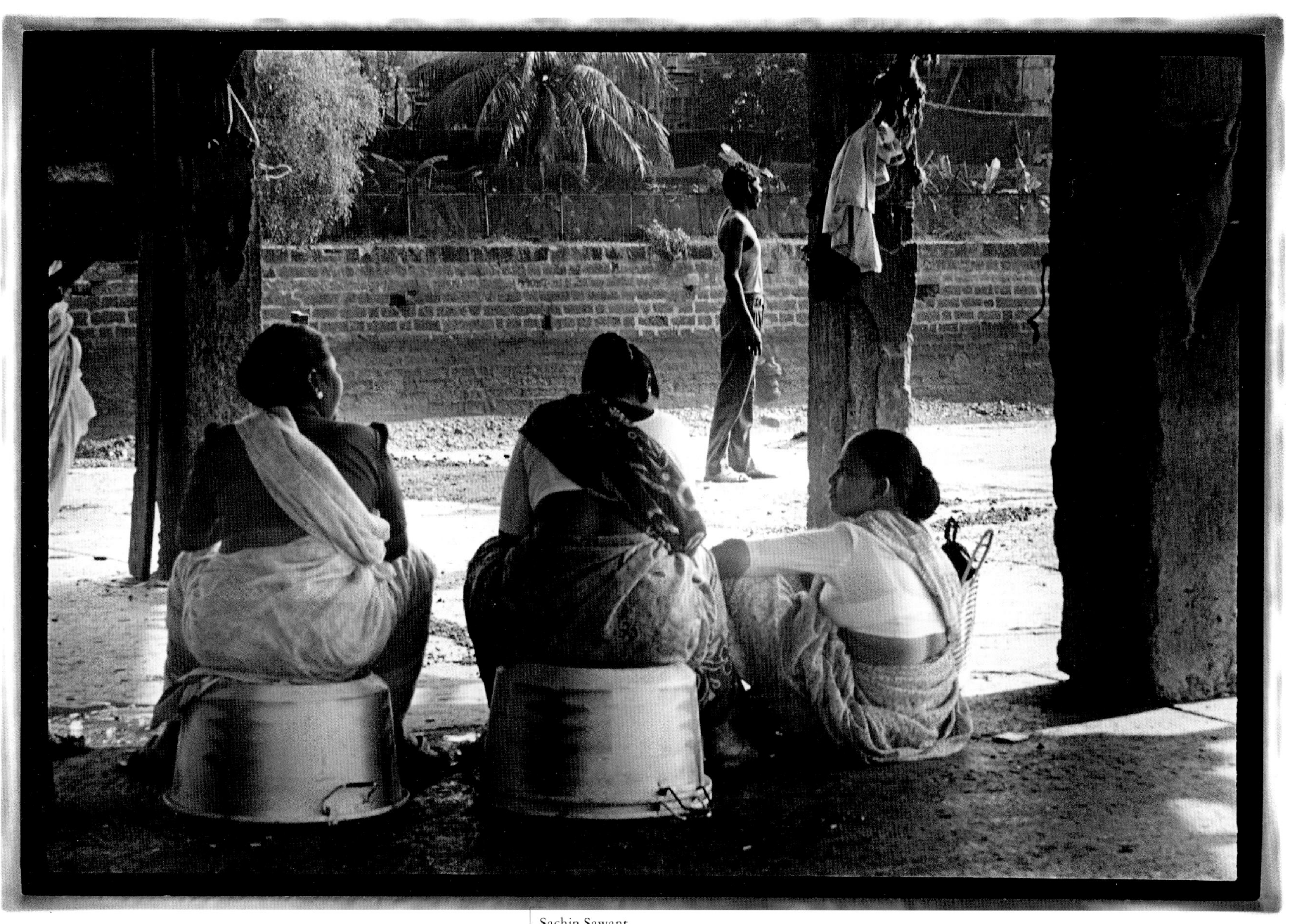

Sachin Sawant
Sassoon Docks, Colaba.

Yamini Hule
Ferry Wharf (Bhaucha Dhakka)
Dockyard Road.

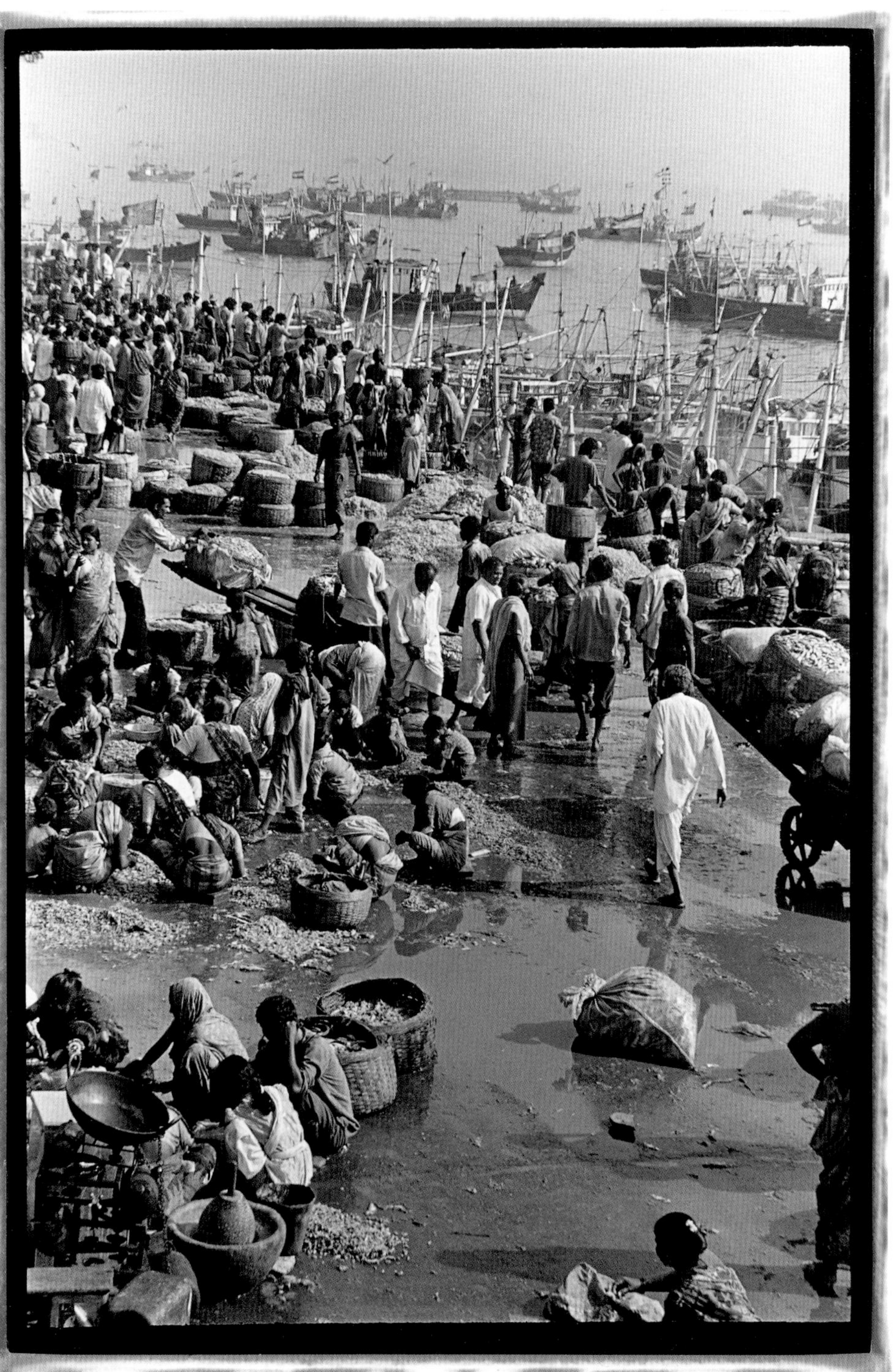

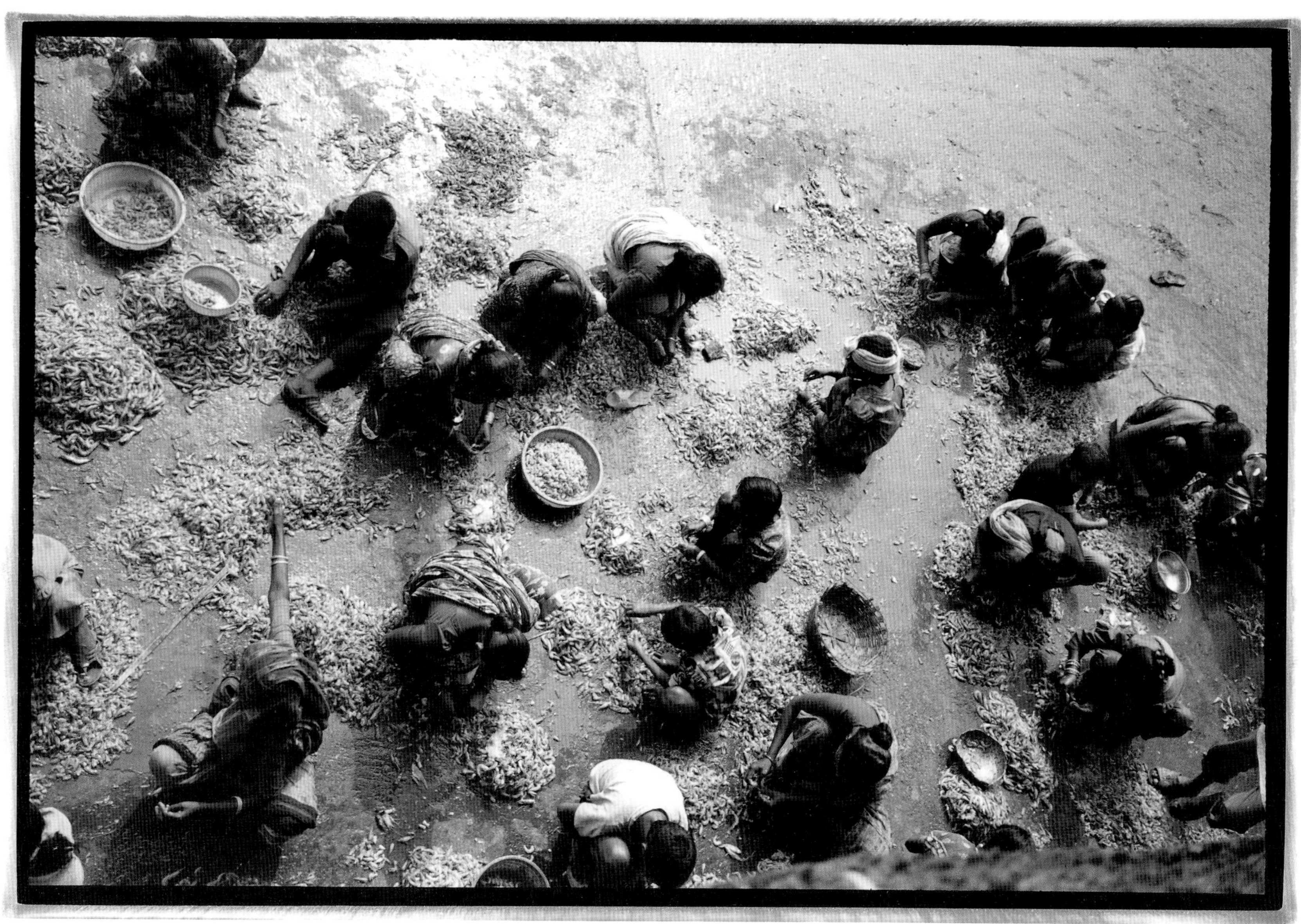

Vinit Chauhan

Ferry Wharf, (Bhaucha Dhakka) Dockyard Road.

Mumbai is a noisy city, but there are tiny corners where one can find peace.

Vinit Chauhan

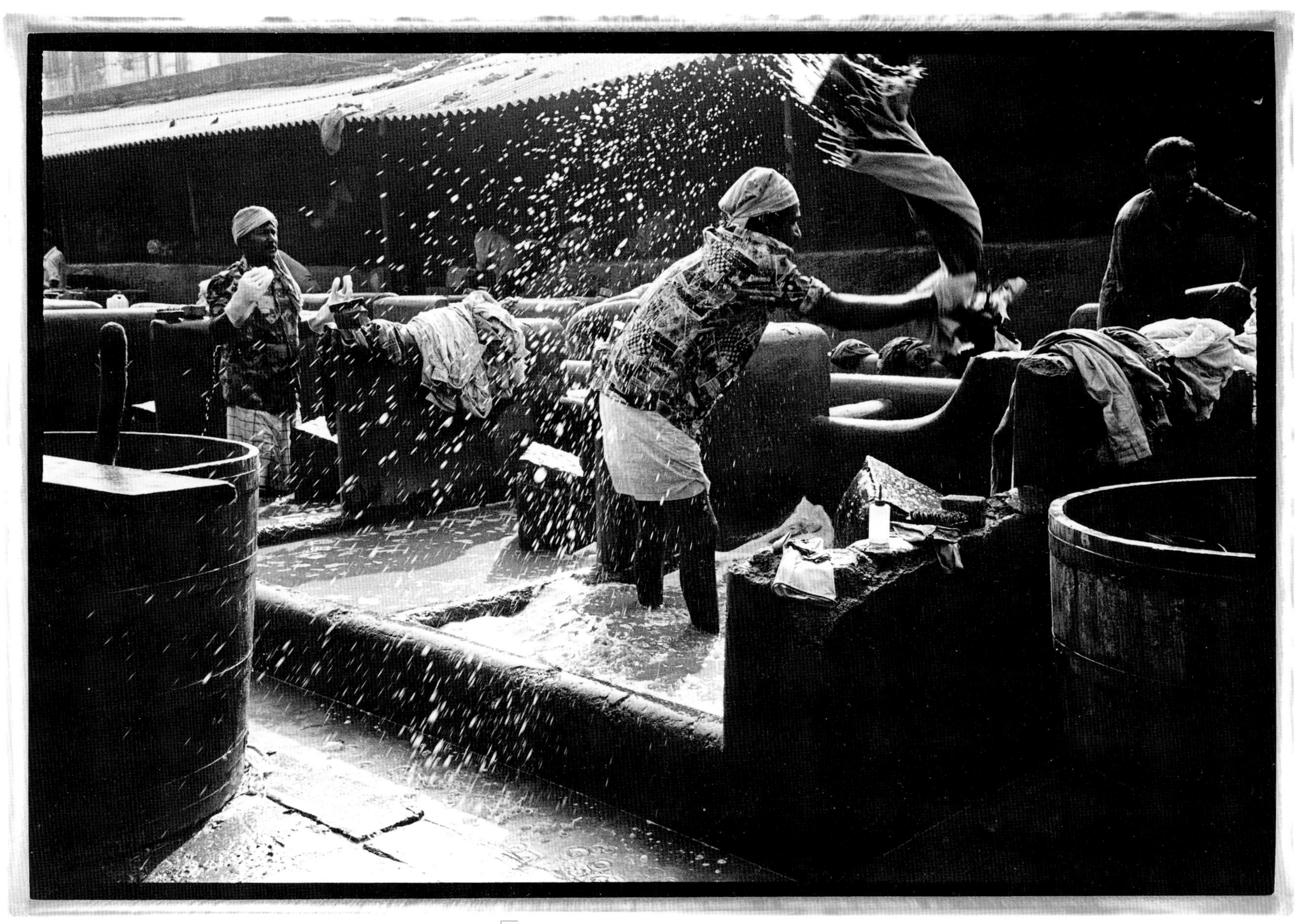

Asir Mulla
Mahalaxmi Dhobi Ghat, Mahalaxmi.

लैंडमार्क क्या है? लैंडमार्क वह है जिसे हम रोज़ आते-जाते शायद देखें भी नहीं, लेकिन अगर वह अचानक एक दिन न रहे तो कुछ कमी सी महसूस होगी.

A landmark is something you perhaps are not even aware of sometimes, until suddenly one day it isn't there — you then feel a personal loss.

Vinit Chauhan

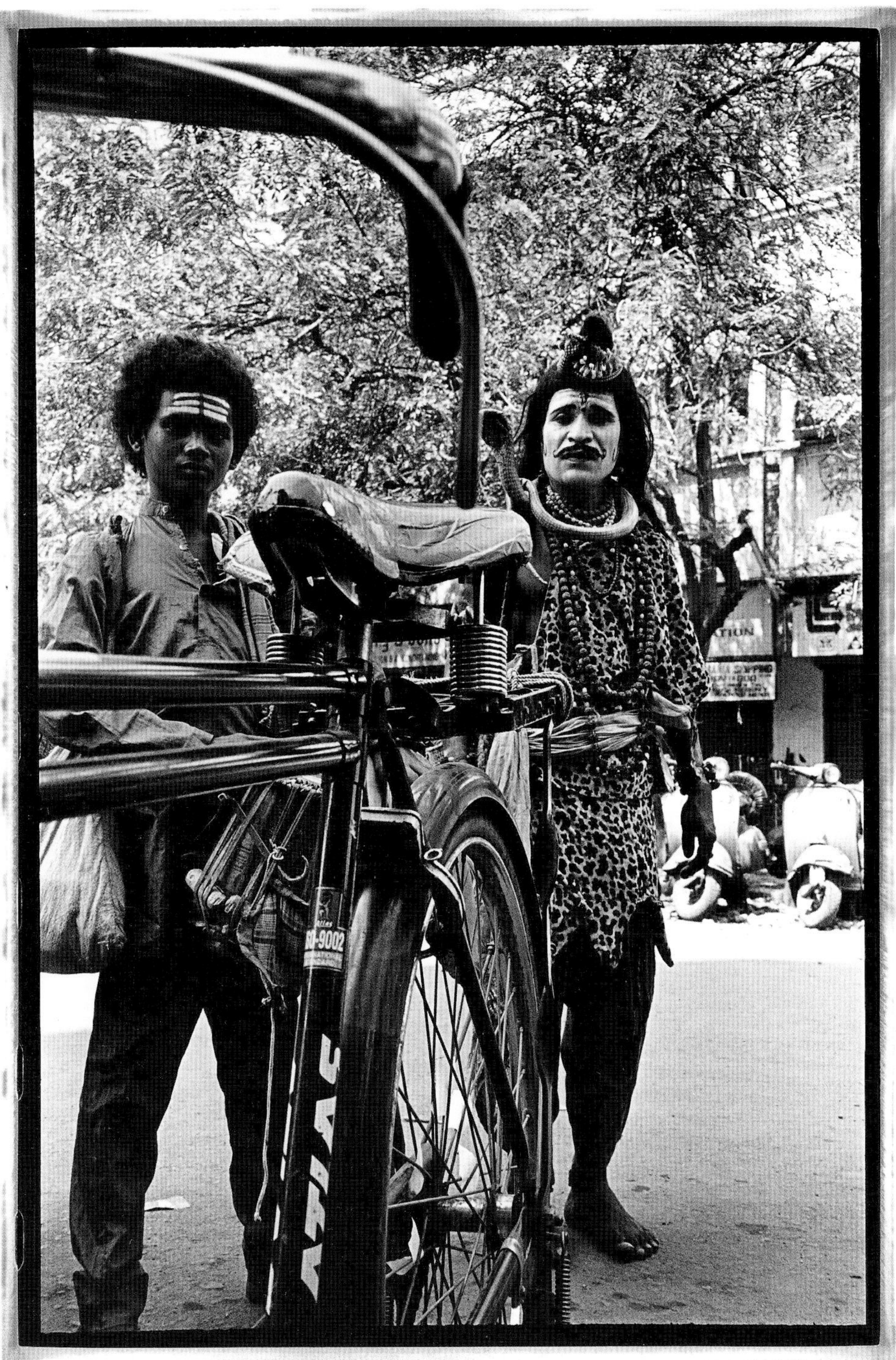

Nicole D'Souza
Shahid Bhagatsingh Marg, Colaba.

I don't particularly spend time in the park, but, like I can't imagine losing it.

Vernon Fernandes

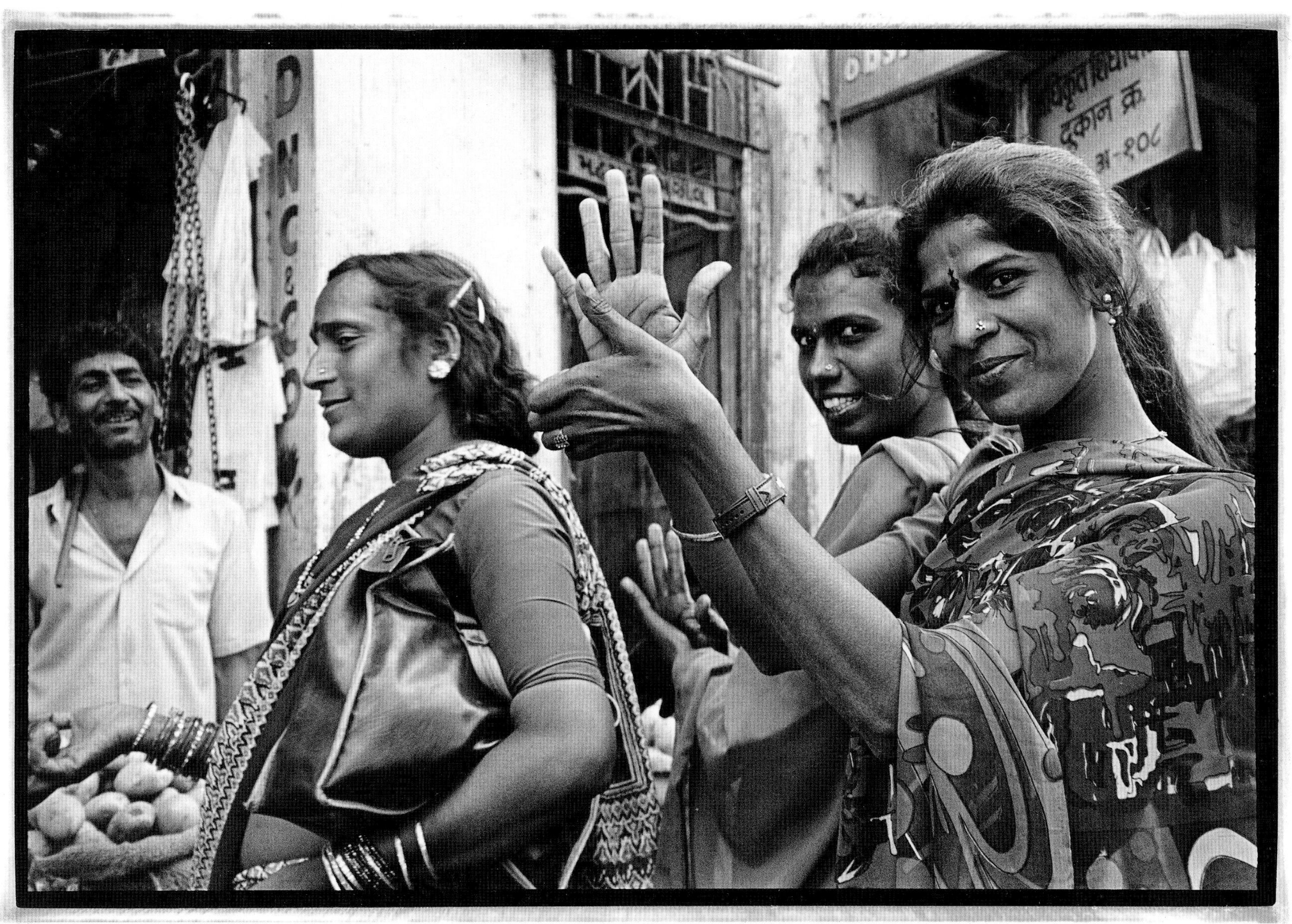

Yamini Hule

Byculla Market, Dr. Babasaheb Ambedkar Road.

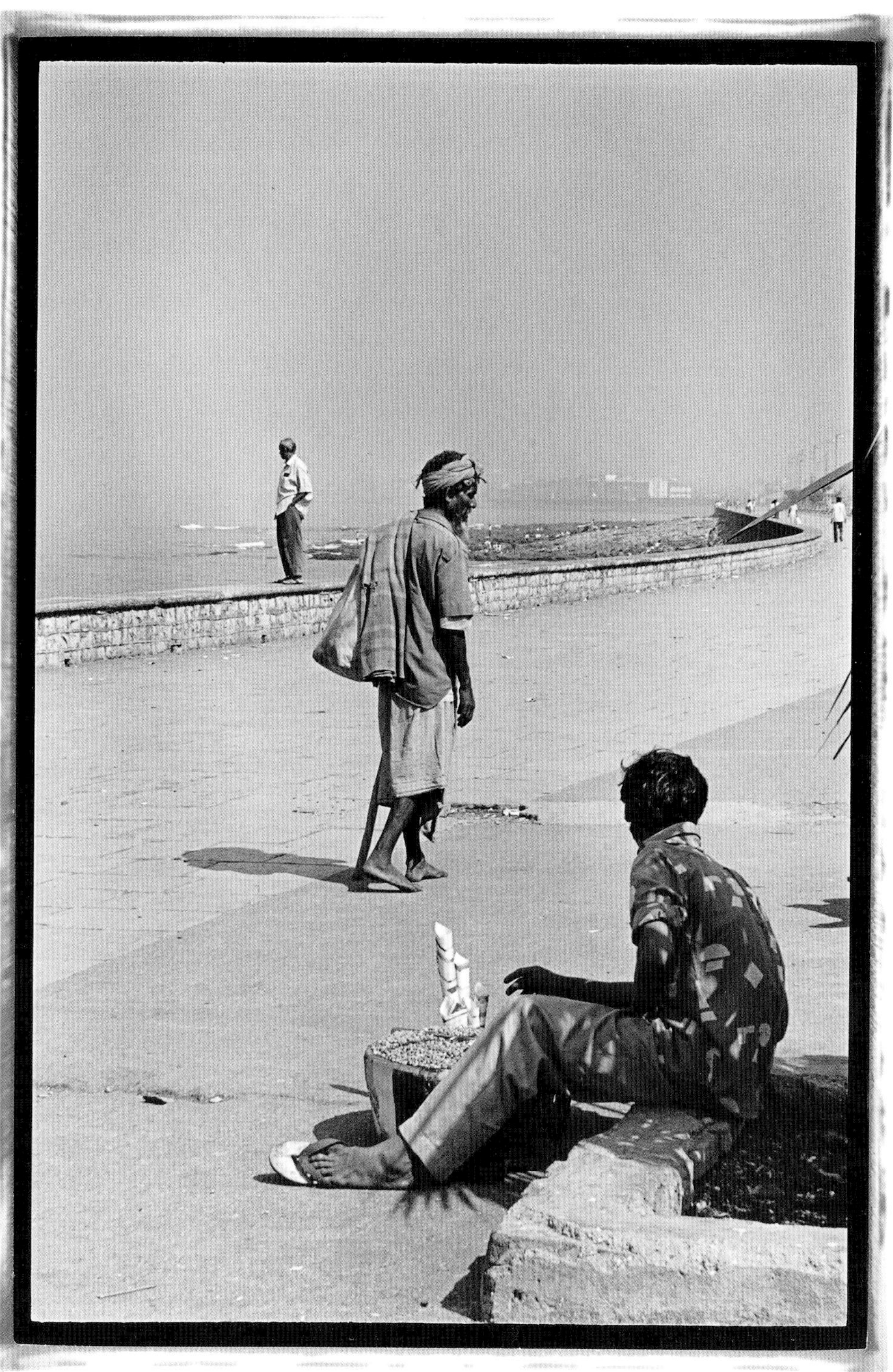

Vernon Fernandes
Worli Sea Face,
Maulana Abdul Gaffarkhan Road.

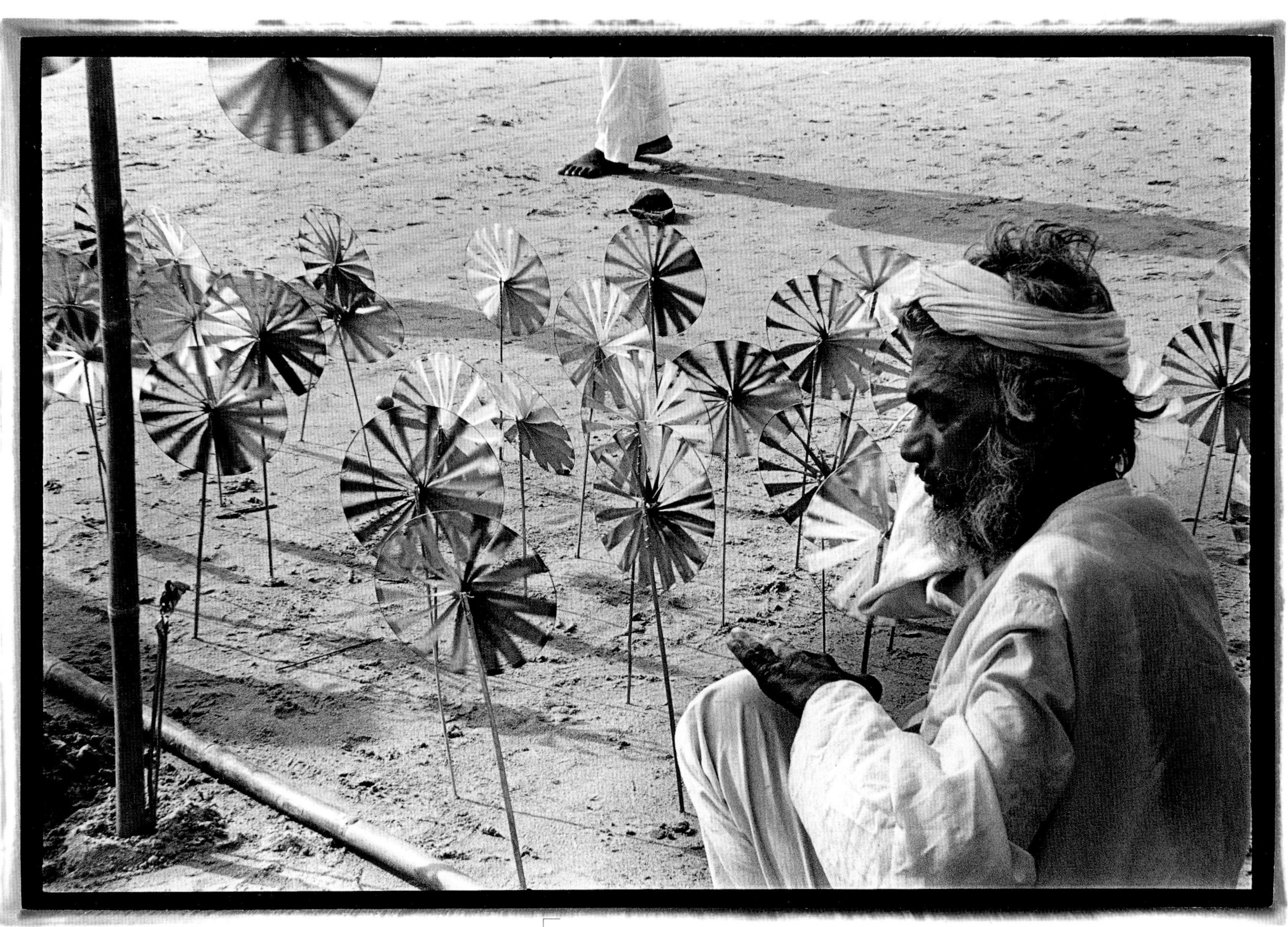

Nivedita Magar
Juhu Beach, Juhu.

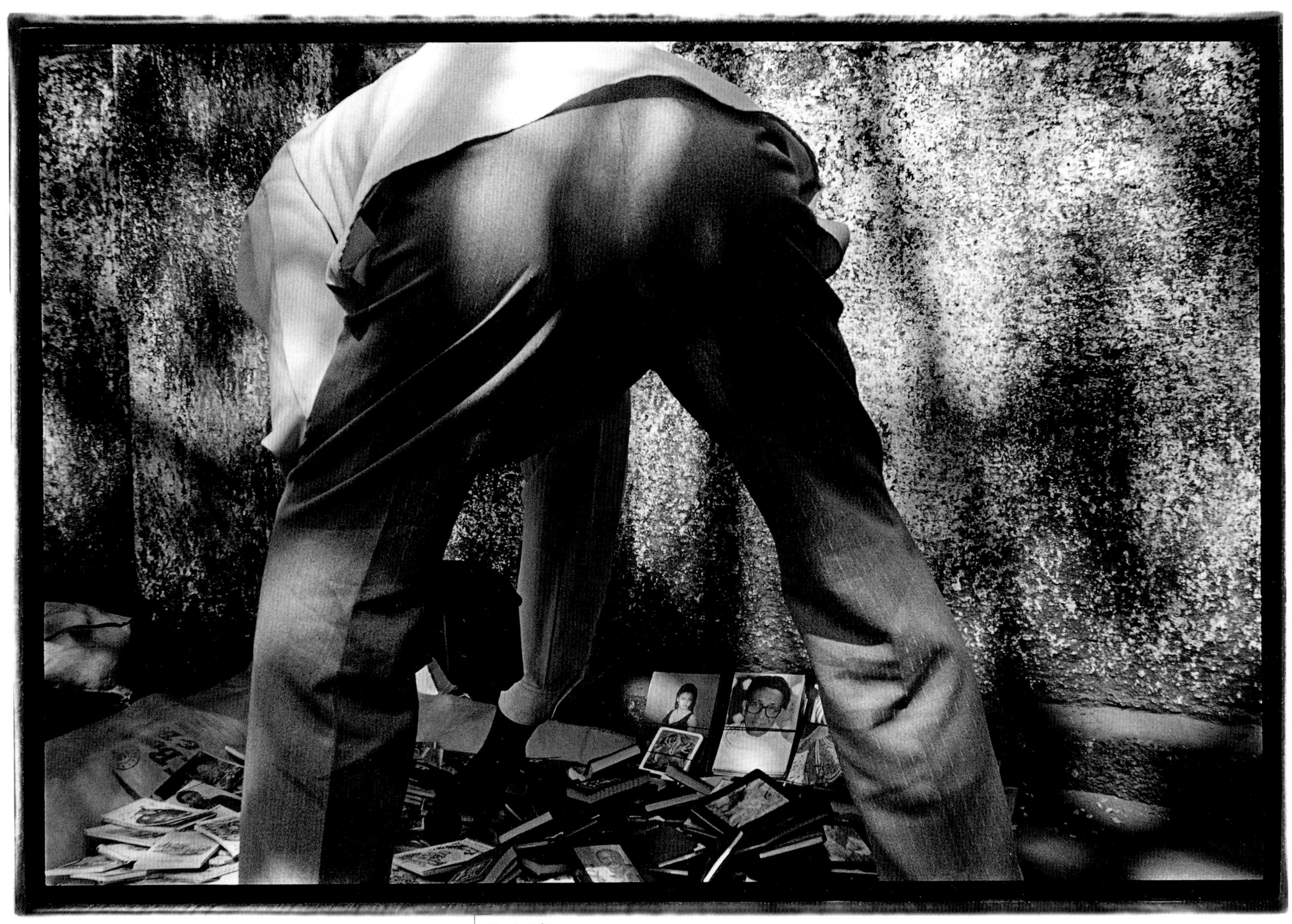

Nicole D'Souza
Outside St. Xavier's College, Mahapalika Marg.

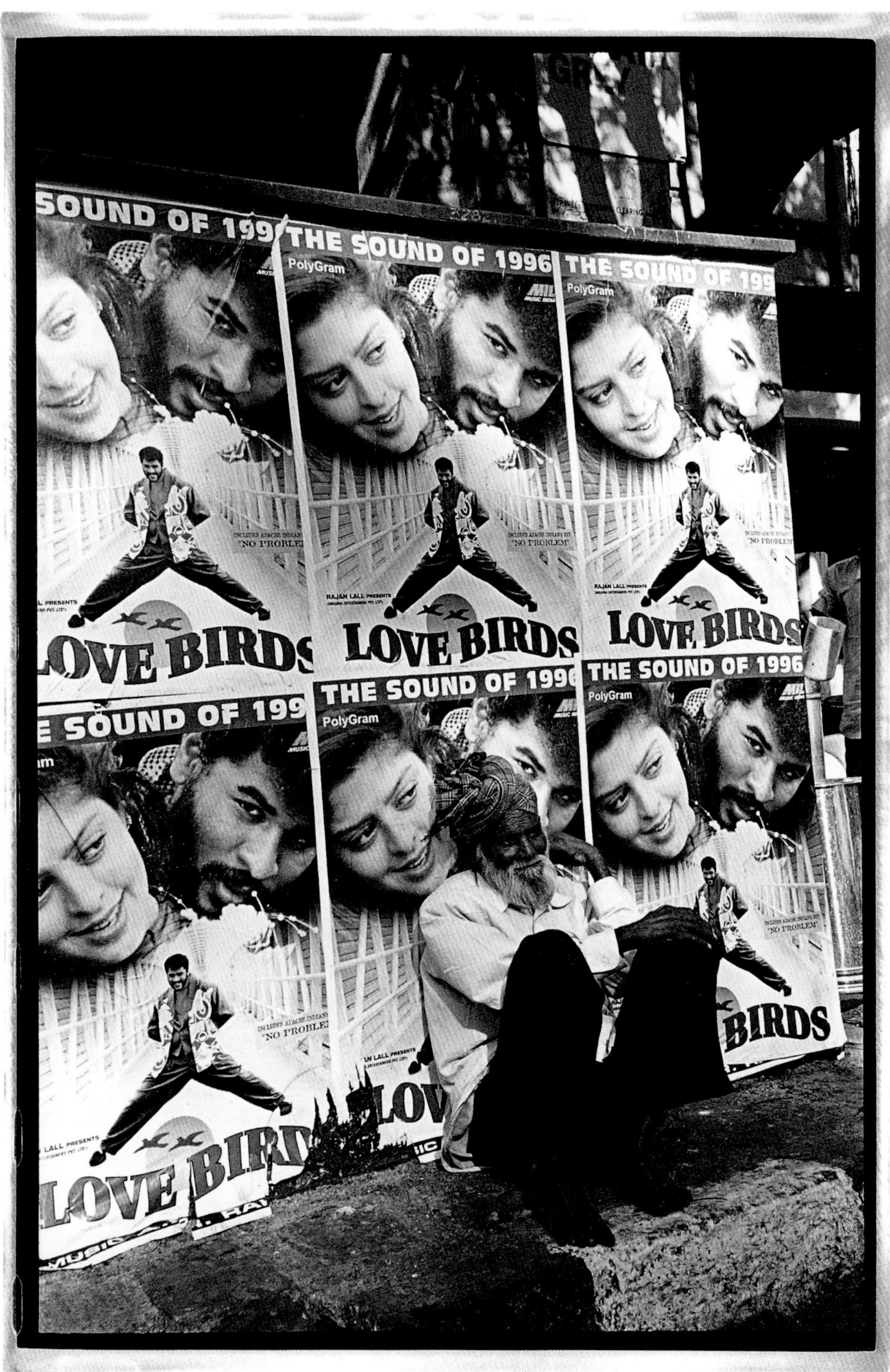

Anitha Balachandran
Outside Rhythm House, Dubash Marg.

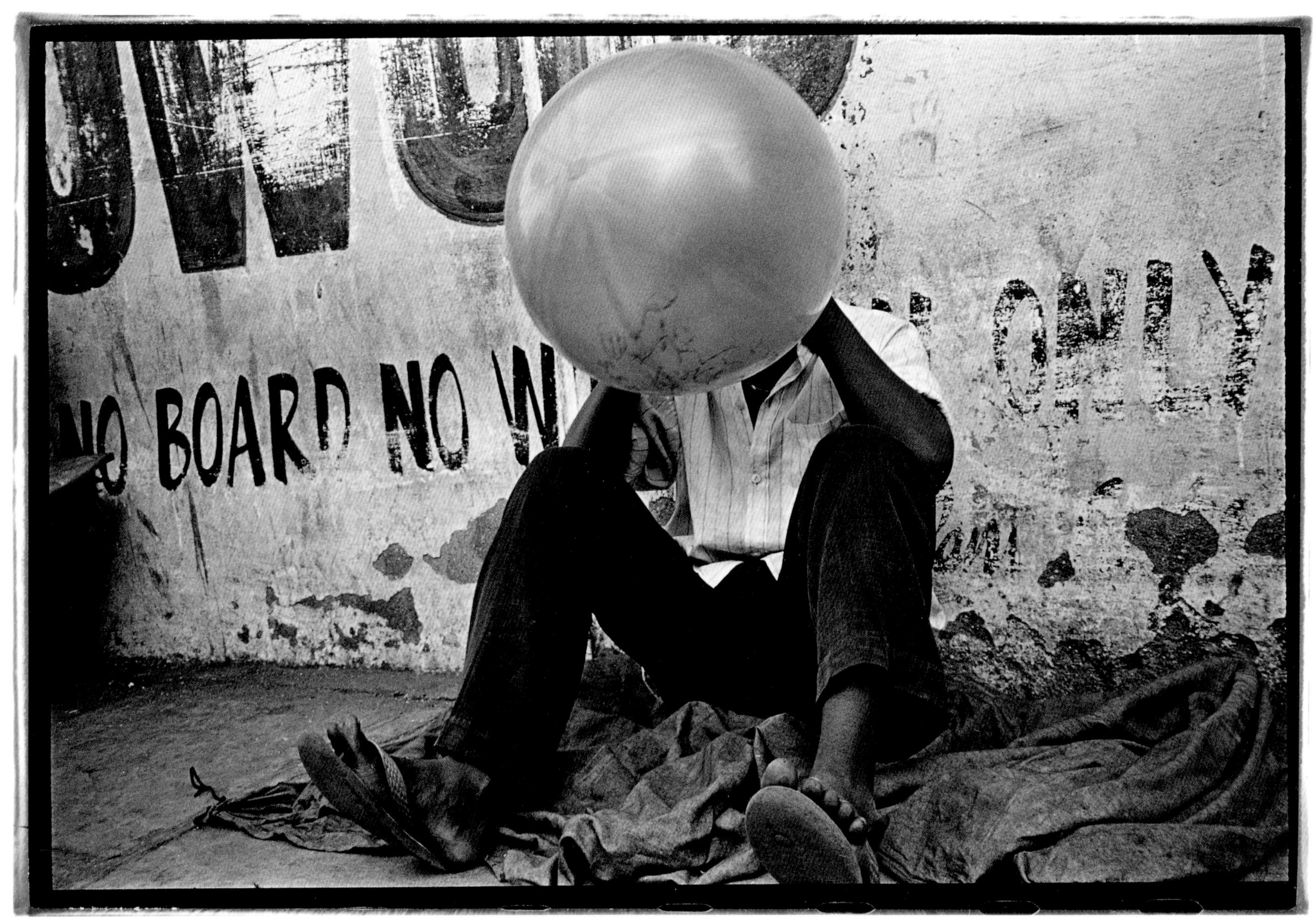

Anitha Balachandran
Cooperage Maidan, Madame Cama Road, Colaba.

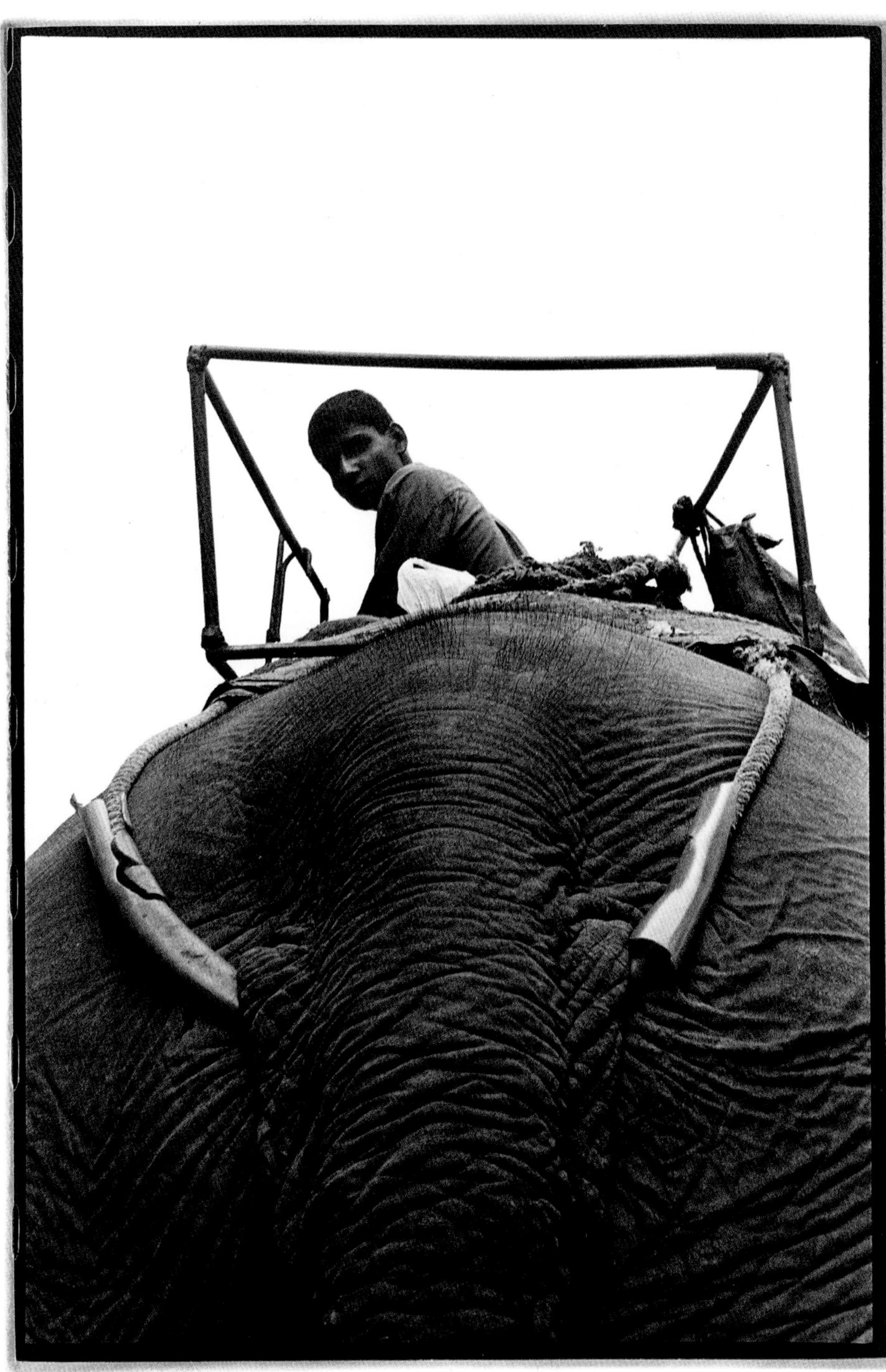

Bikram Mitra
Bhuleshwar Road, Bhuleshwar.

To me a landmark is something I can recognise myself by.

What gives Mumbai the finishing touch are the people. They create and break the landmark. The thing that sets Mumbai apart from the "foreign" is the life our landmarks have. Everything here is living, right from your garbage infested with insects to your posh flats with Picasso paintings. However, most landmarks are being destroyed by men—no care for the future generation to be able to look upon with pride and say "this is my country." I hope that these photographs in the future make an impact on those youngsters who missed the opportunity to see what could have been theirs, to preserve what will be their children's. For me the ordinary 'channawalla', the 'bhelpuriwalla', the hand-cart pullers are all landmarks. Something that will vanish with technology, but one landmark that will never go is the life and the perseverance of all Mumbaiites to pull through as seen in the bomb blasts and riots.

I'm one of them. Nicole D'Souza

to be able to say to myself I am still a Mumbaiite.

It has to be there each morning when I get up,

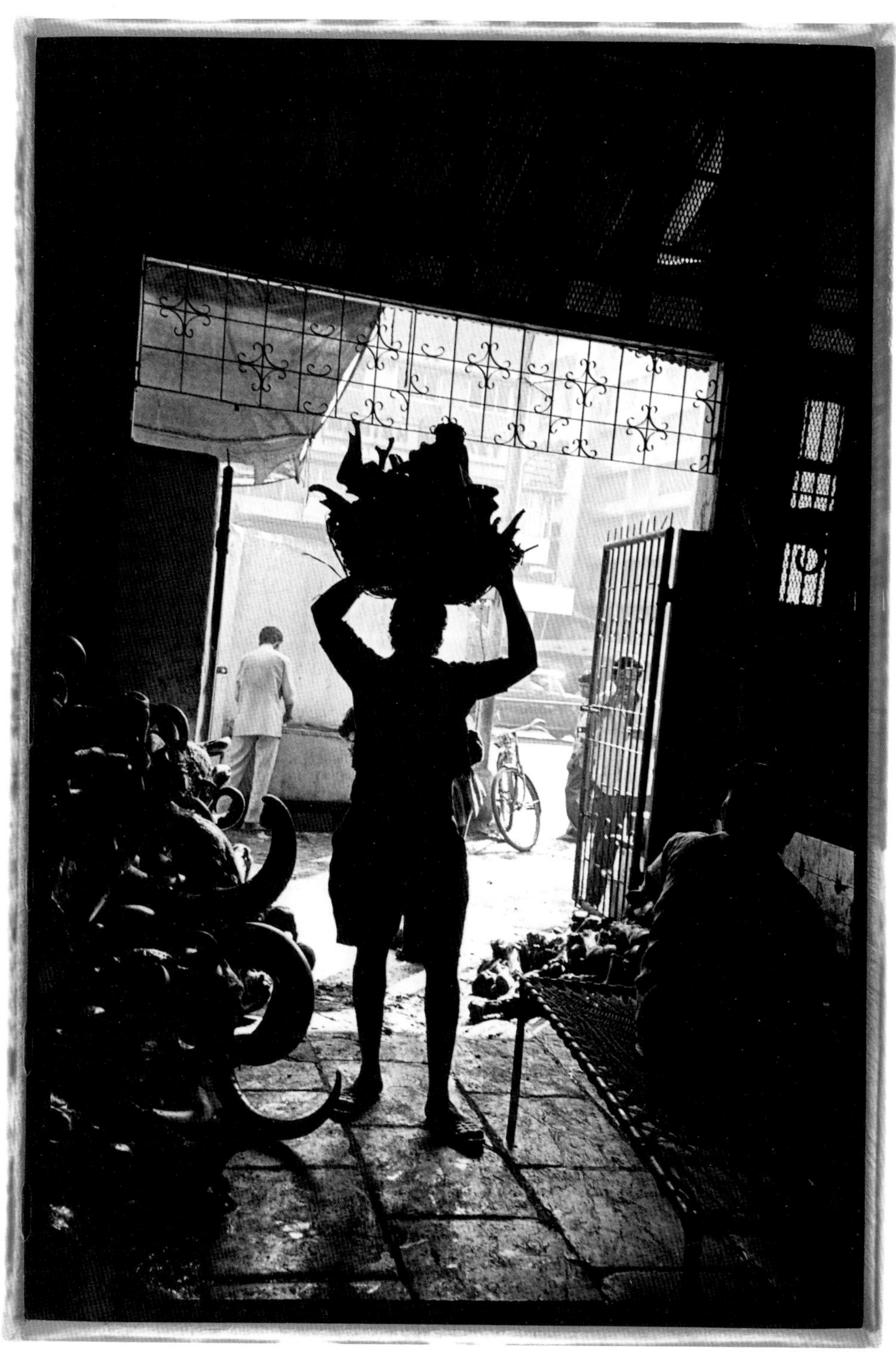

Vernon Fernandes
Mahatma Phule Market (Crawford Market),
Palton Road.

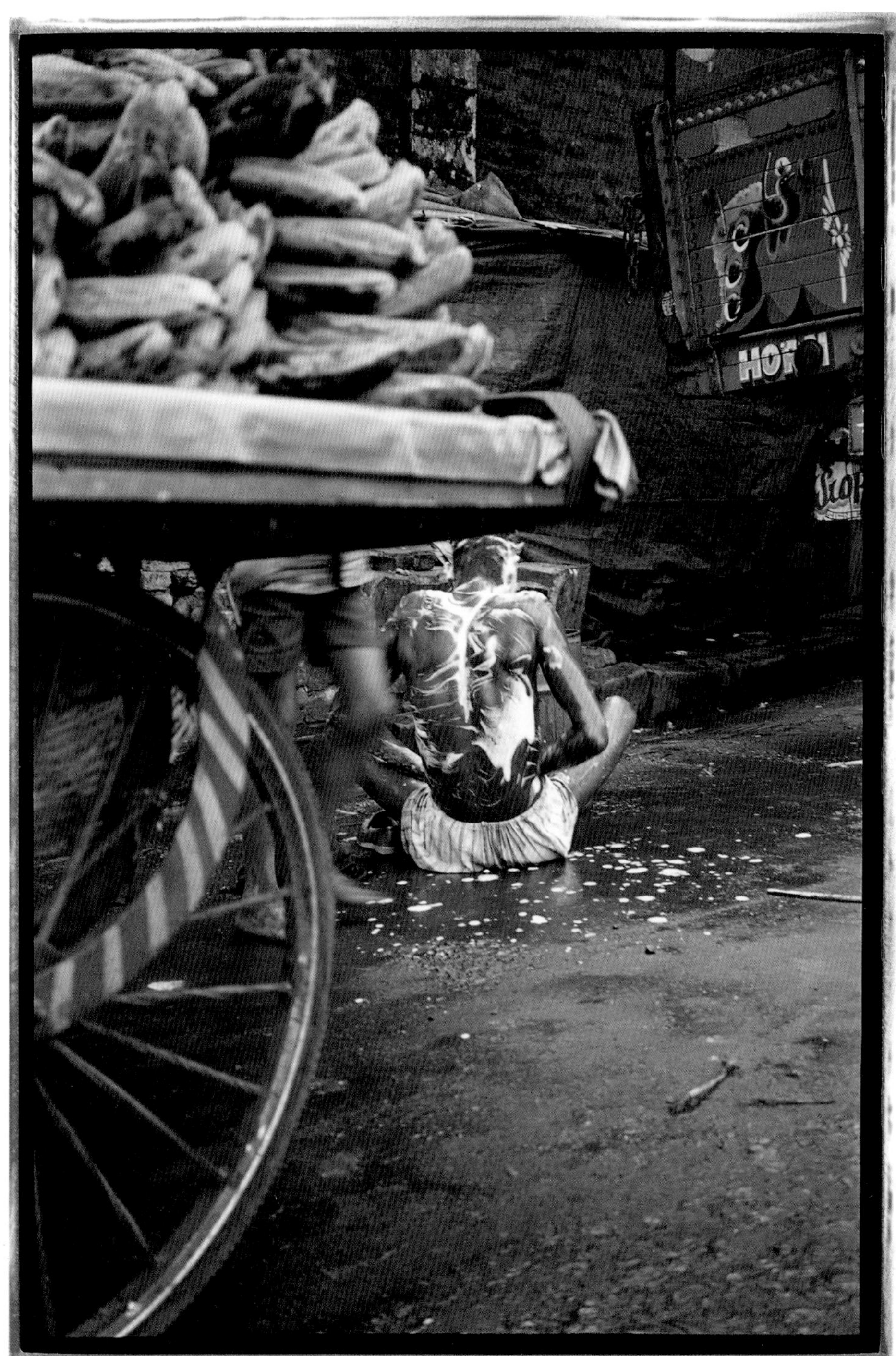

Nicole D'Souza
Between the warehouses, P. D'Mello Road.

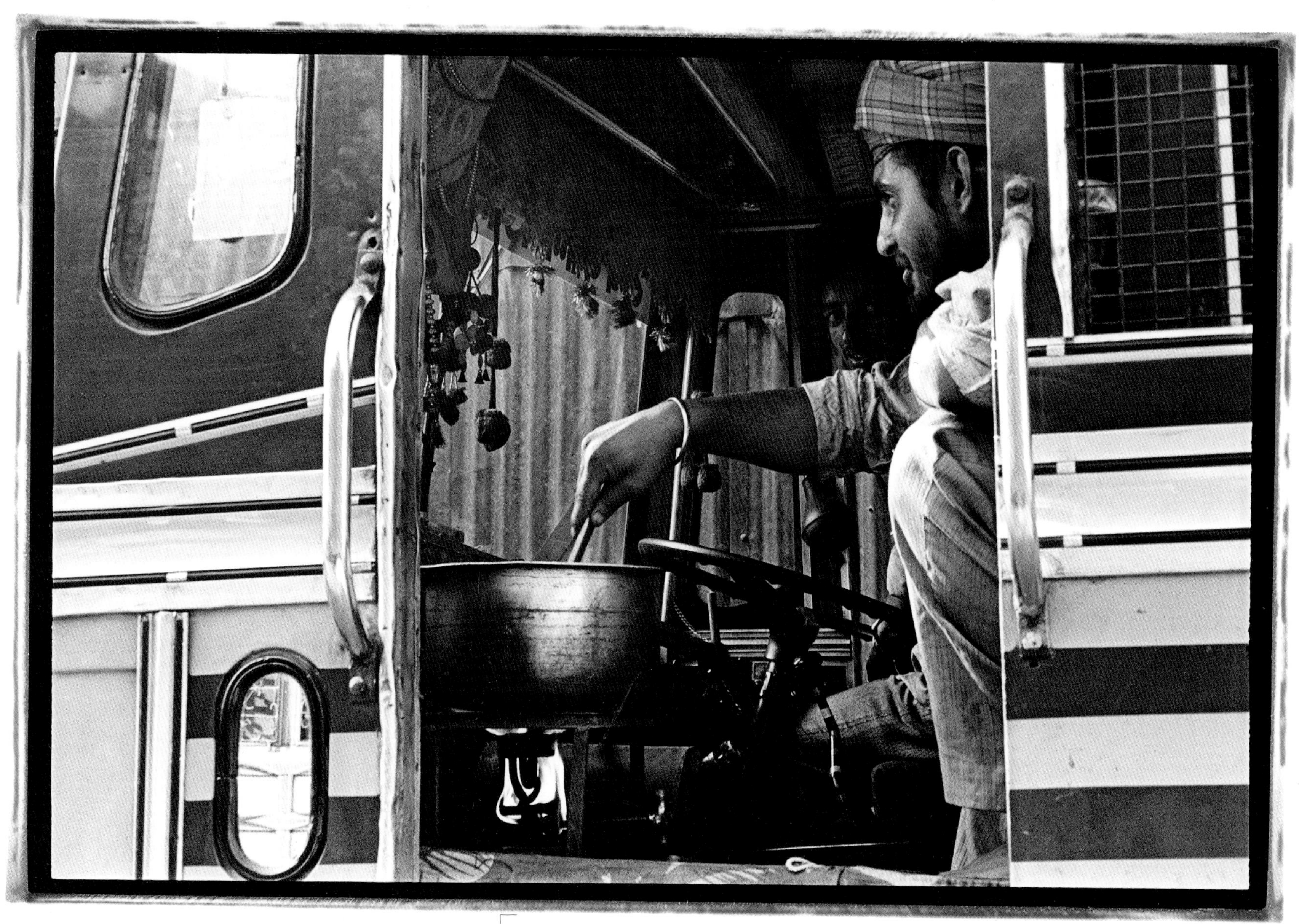

Yamini Hule

Warehouse, P. D'Mello Road, Masjid.

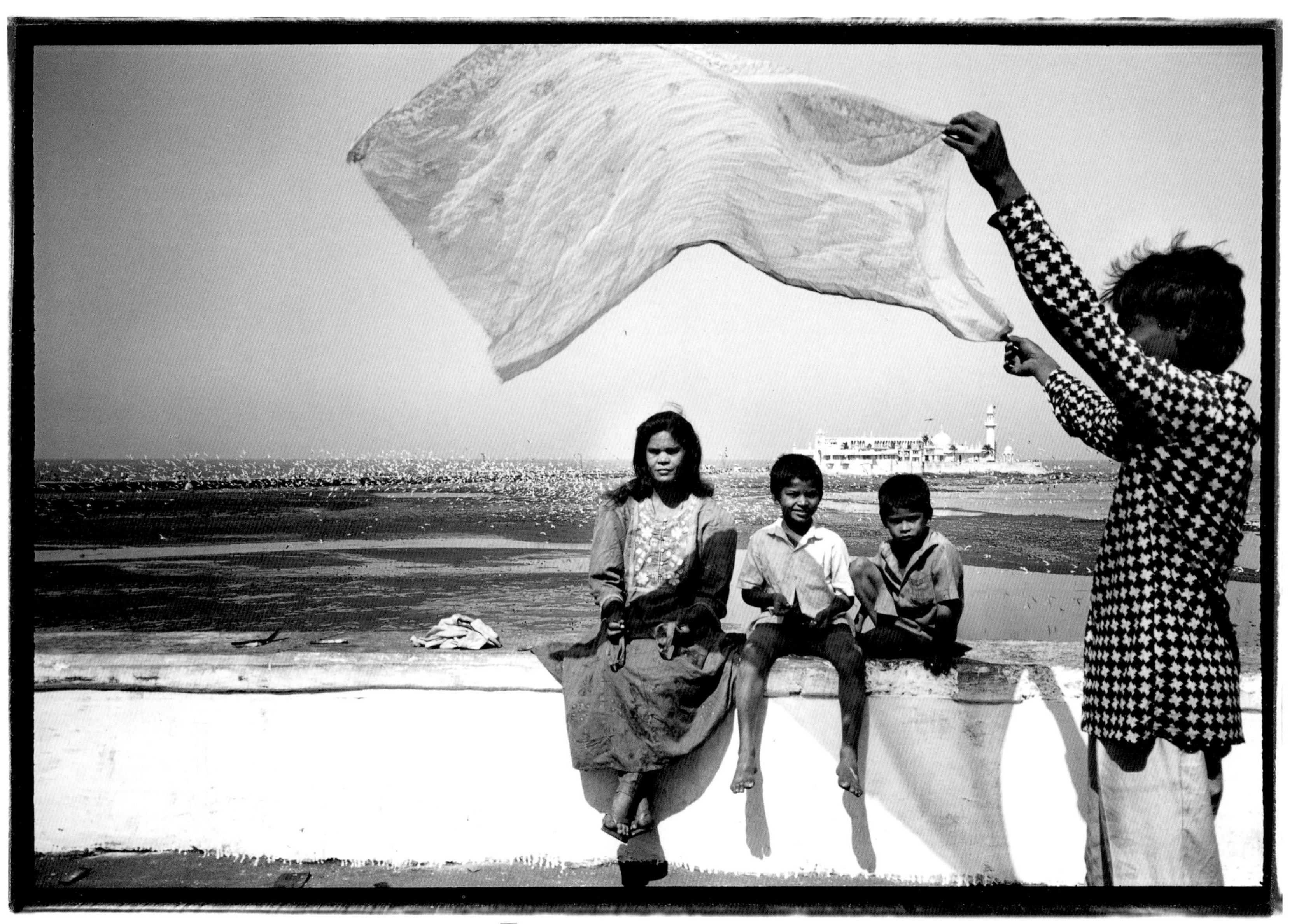

Nivedita Magar
Haji Ali, Lala Lajpatrai Marg.

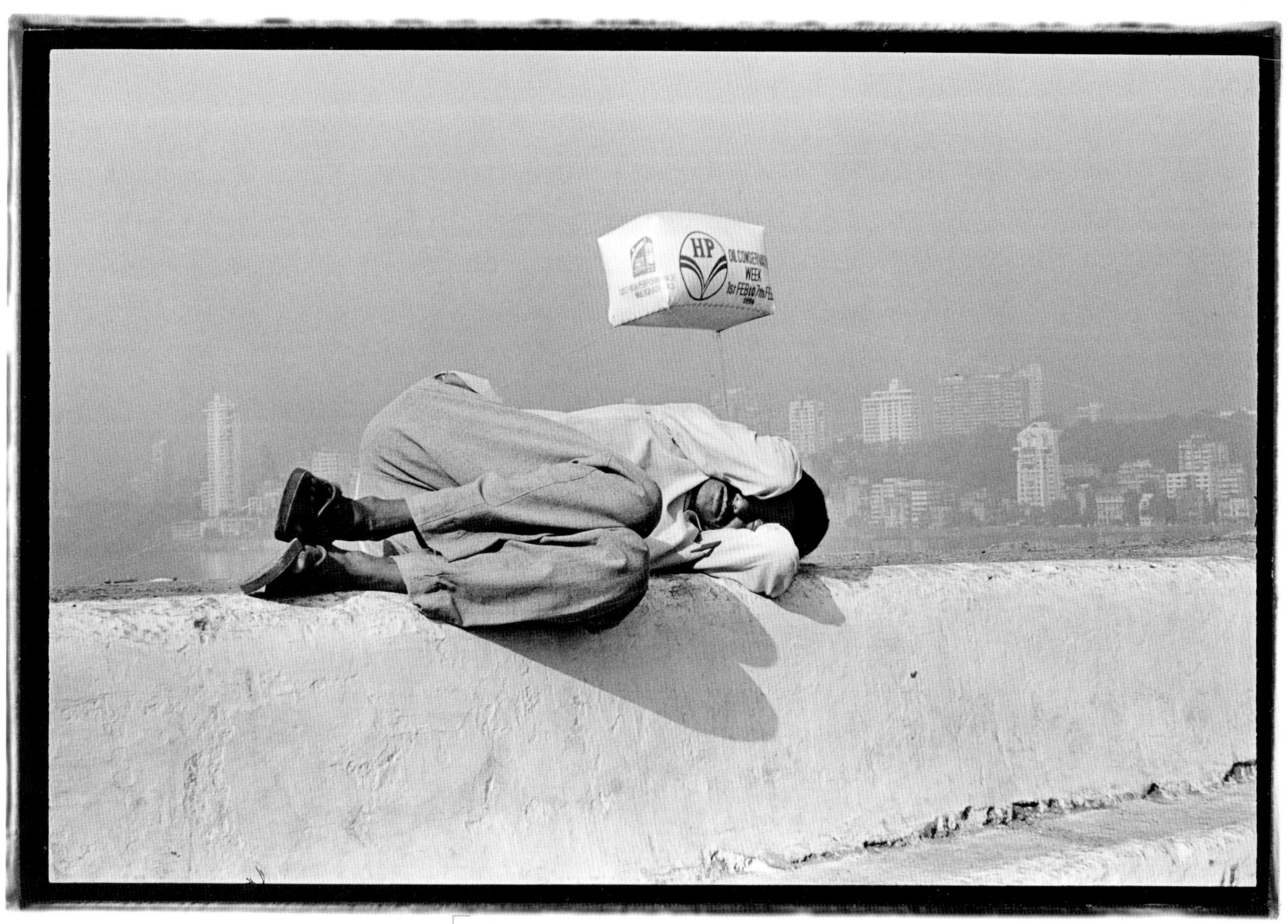

Anitha Balachandran

Marine Drive, Netaji Subhash Chandra Bose Road.

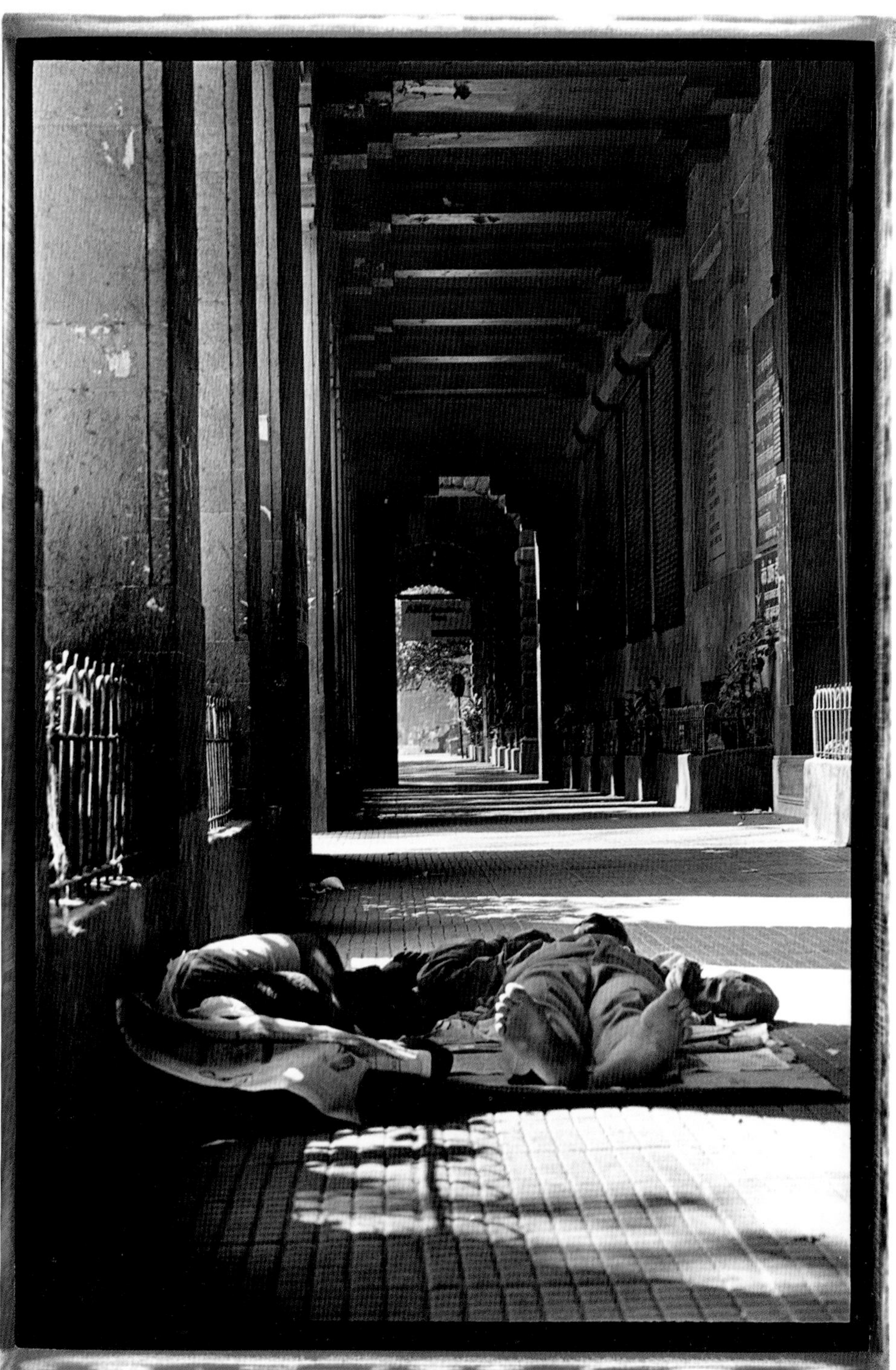

Vinit Chauhan
ANZ Grindlays Bank,
Dadabhai Navroji Road.

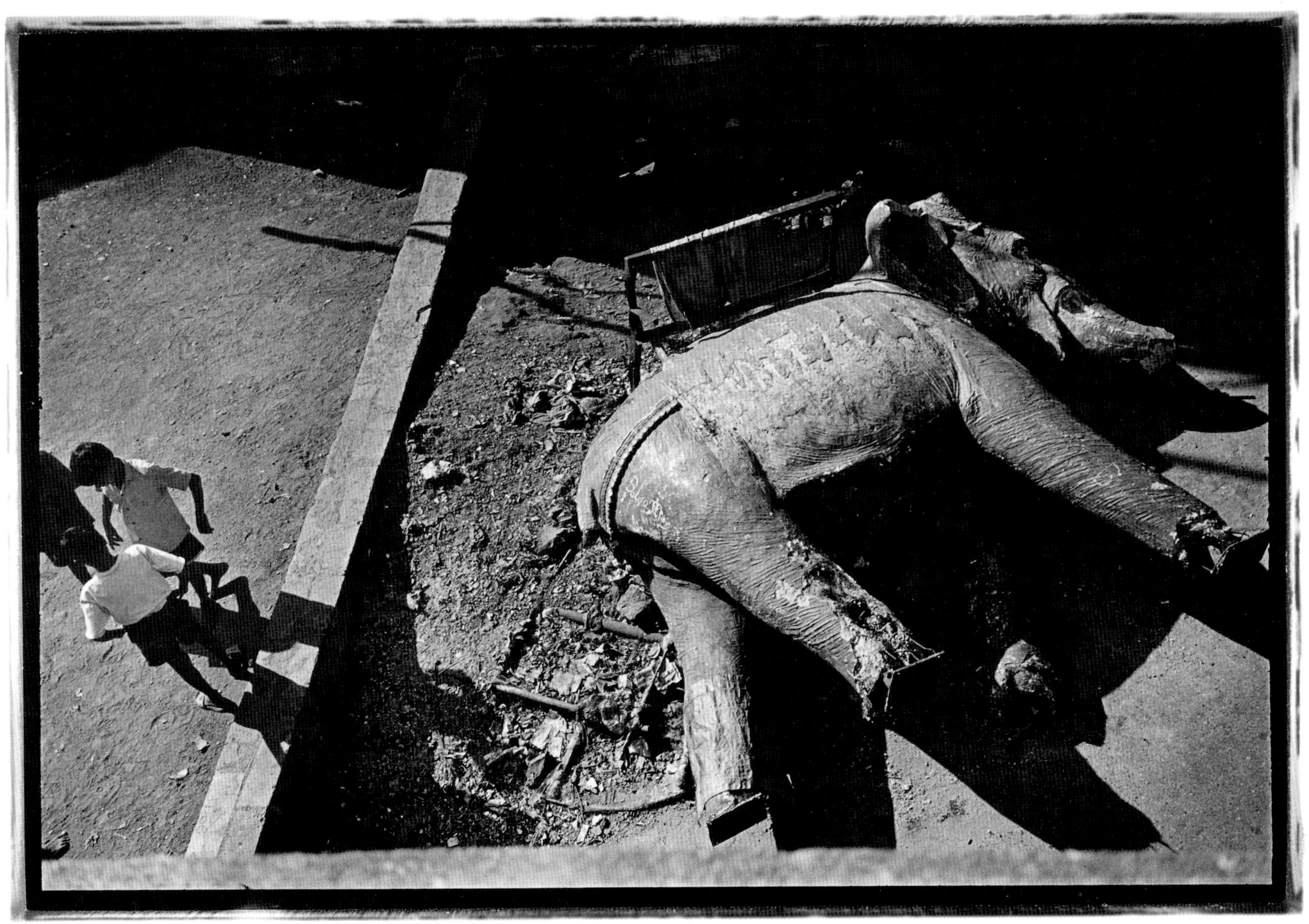

Anitha Balachandran
Mahalaxmi Bridge, near Gadge Maharaj Chowk.

Curious onlookers are everywhere in Mumbai...when we set up our tripods, we would attract a few and ended up answering more questions than taking pictures.
The streets of Bhuleshwar have always been dirty and crowded, just like many others in Mumbai.
In Mumbai a crowd can include animals too, cats, dogs, cows, bulls...
The subway at Churchgate station is busy, it's sad when children live there, maybe their parents choose to live there; after all, the bigger the crowd, the more the alms.

In the hot sun, I was too tired to get out of the taxi and would rather lazily shoot through the taxi window. I would see children out on the street; the difference was that I had emptied at least four bottles of Pepsi, whereas they had a drink of not so clean water, I had a taxi to sit in, they had the dirty pavement. I was looking forward to a cricket match that was going to be on TV later that evening, they were probably looking forward to a game of marbles. But they were happy and I wasn't.

Bikram Mitra

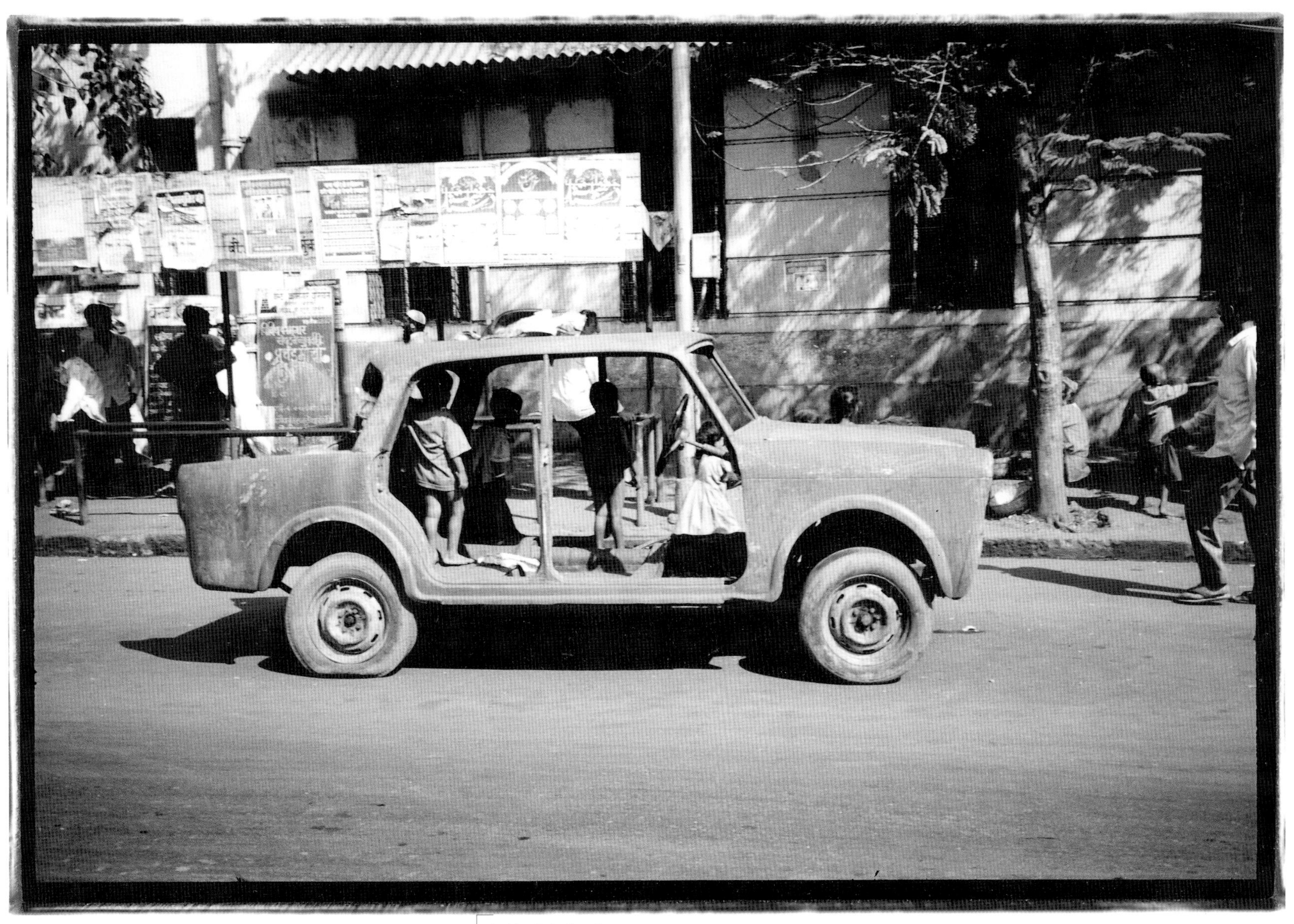

Anitha Balachandran
Maulana Shaukatali Road, Kamatipura.

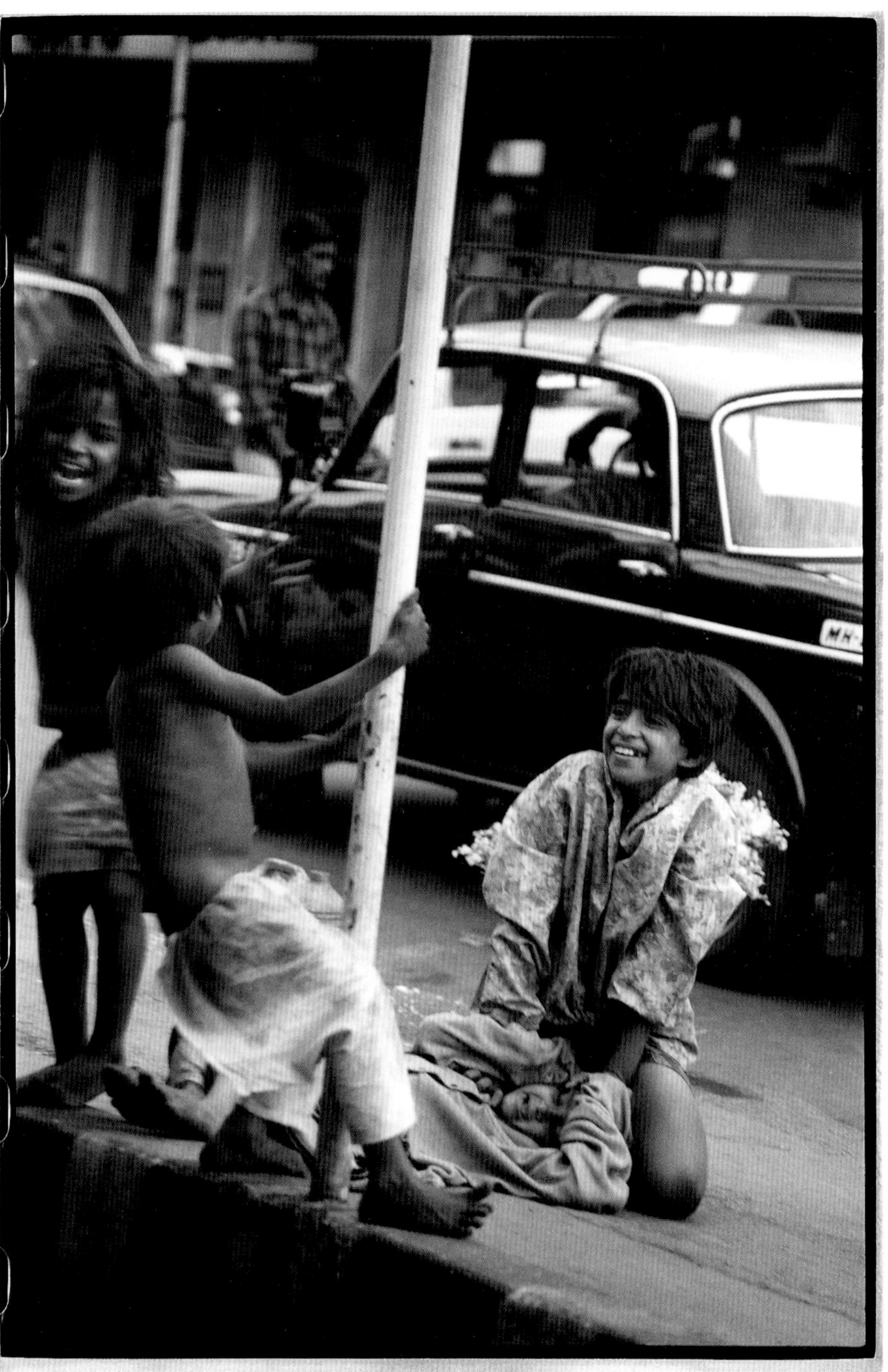

Bikram Mitra
Breach Candy, Bhulabhai Desai Road.

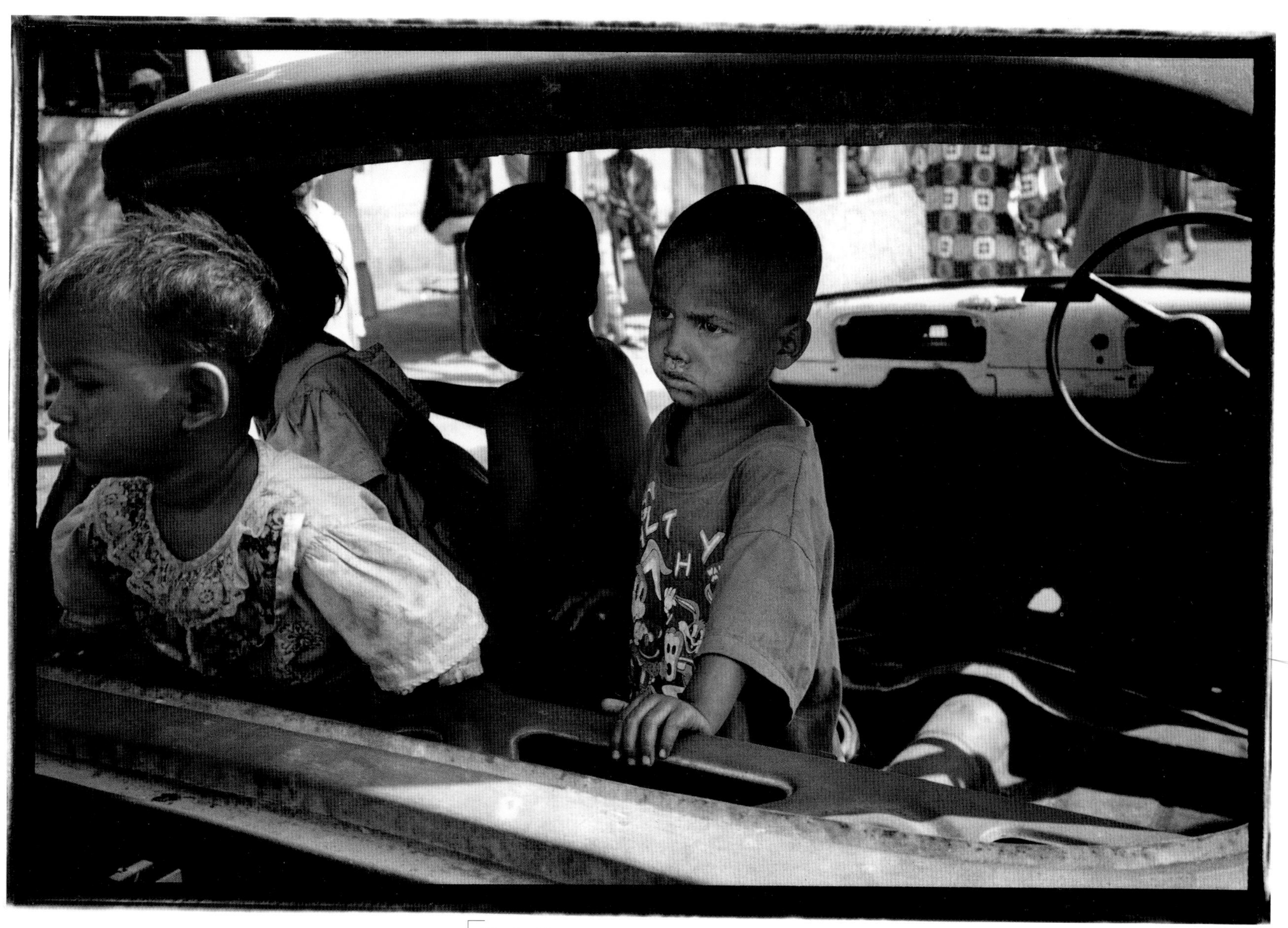

Nivedita Magar
Maulana Shaukatali Road, Kamatipura.

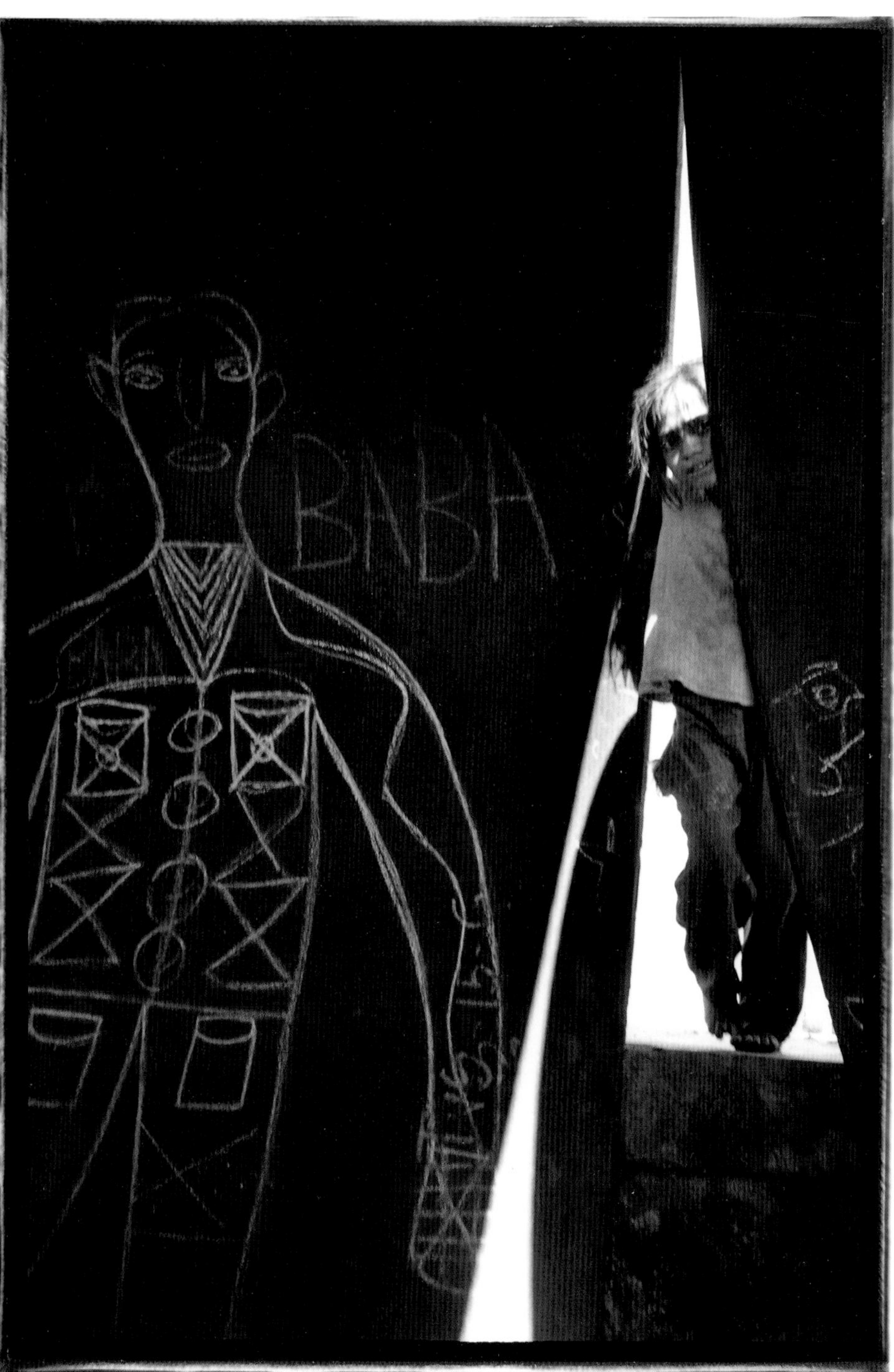

Anitha Balachandran
Western Express Highway, Bandra.

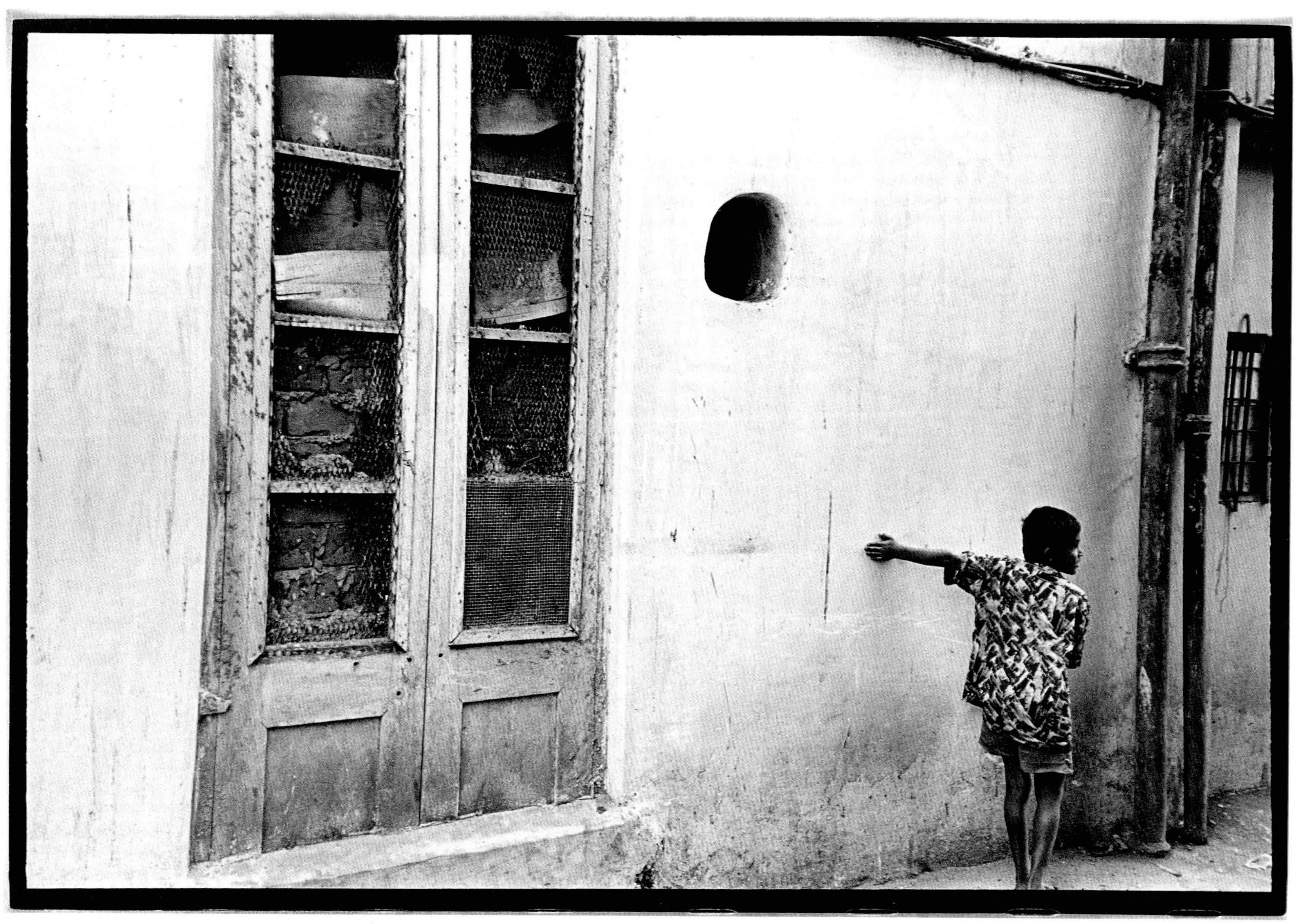

Nivedita Magar
Near Babulnath Temple, Babulnath Road.

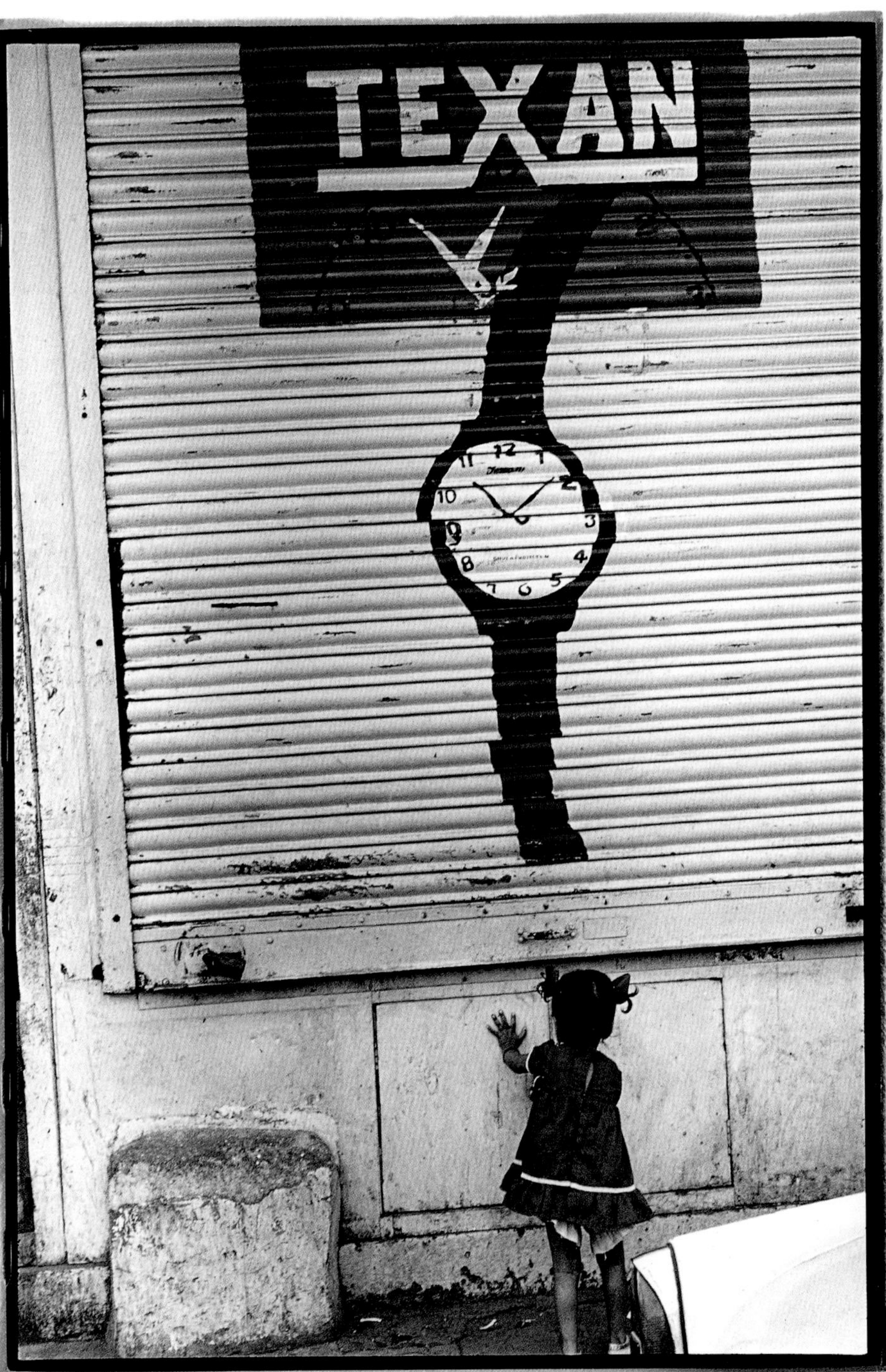

Bikram Mitra
Bhuleshwar Road, Bhuleshwar.

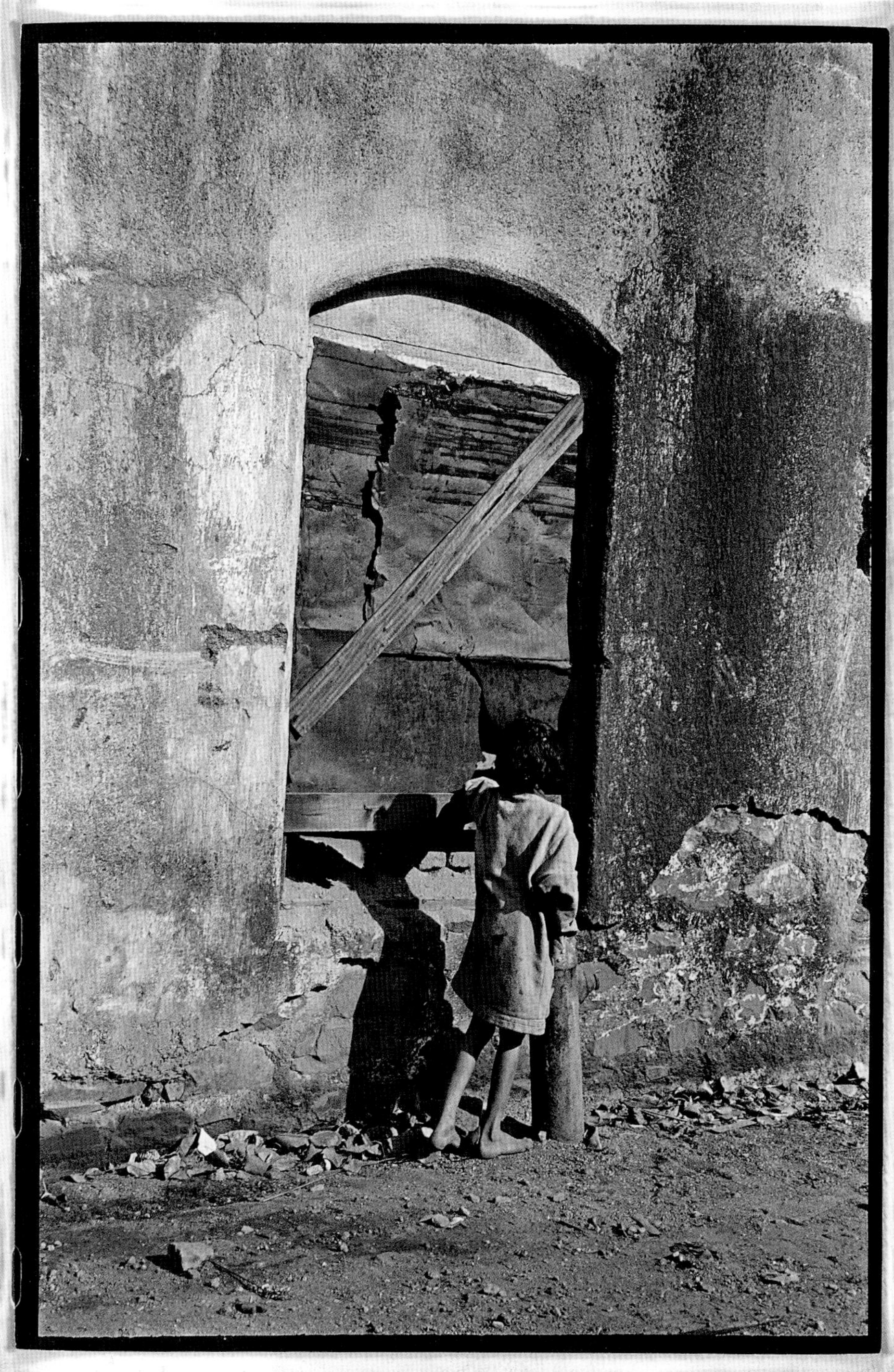

Asir Mulla
Abandoned warehouse, Lower Parel.

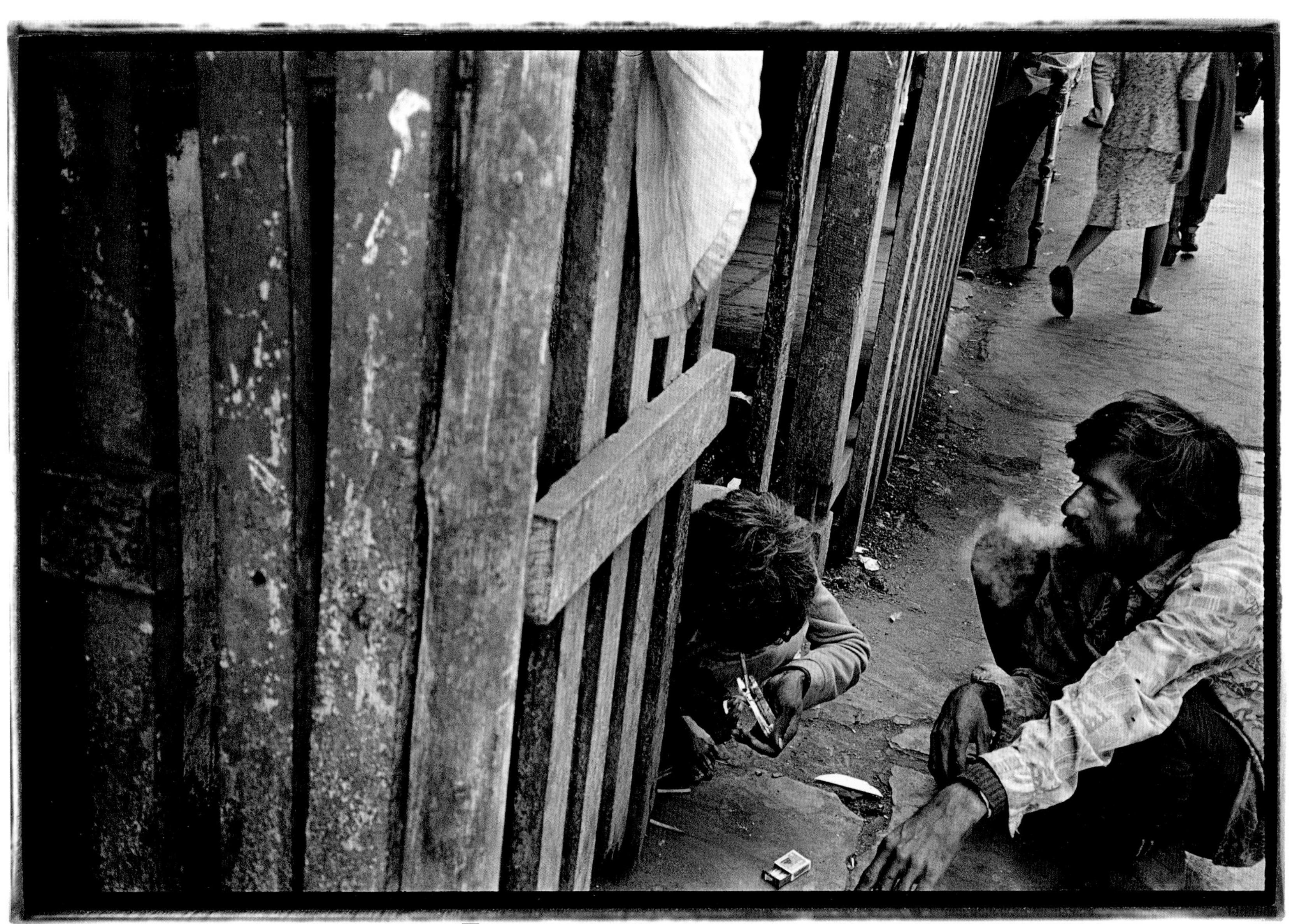

Nivedita Magar
Men smoking brown sugar, Parel Station.

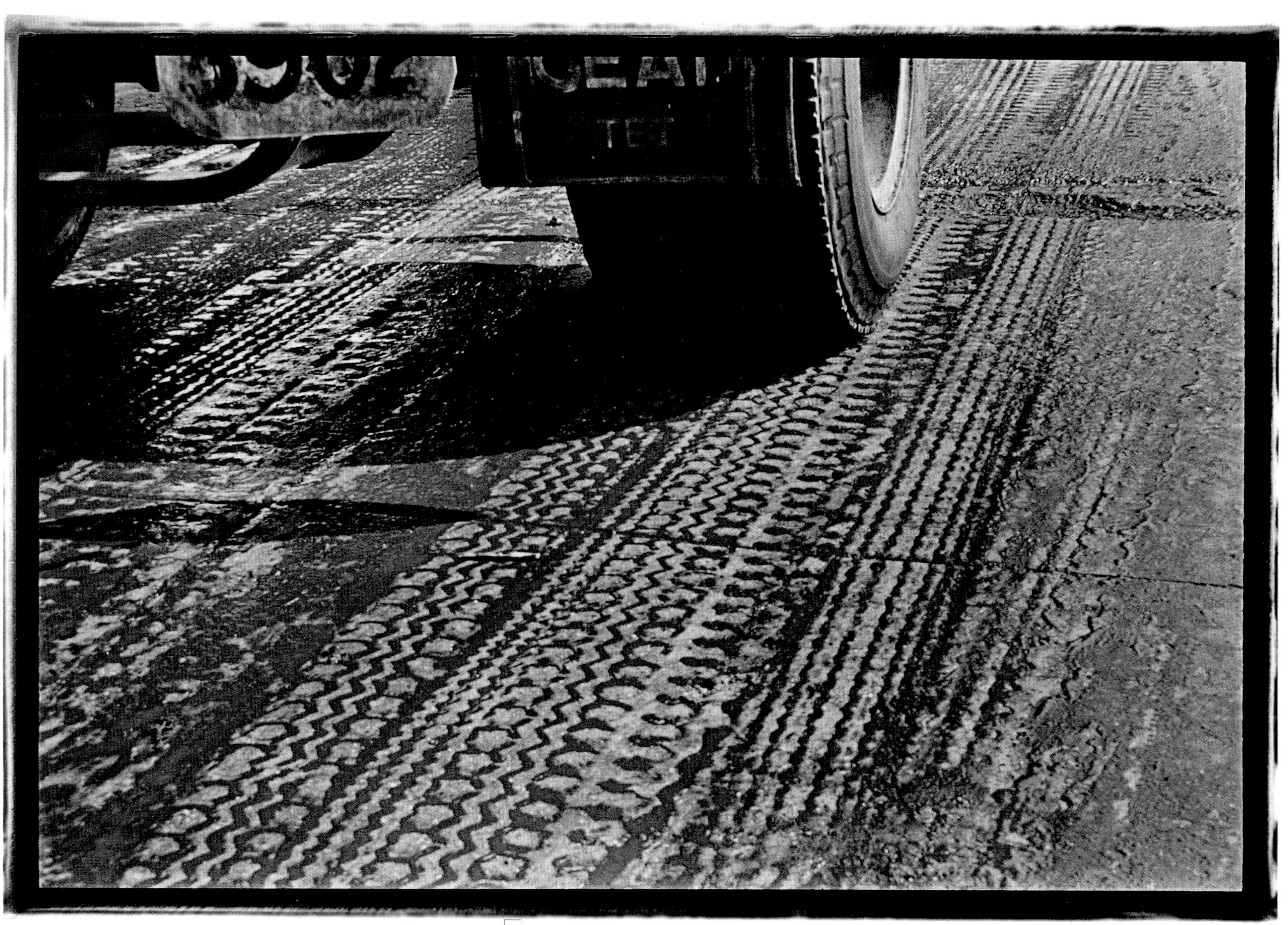

Anitha Balachandran
Ferry Wharf, Dockyard Road.

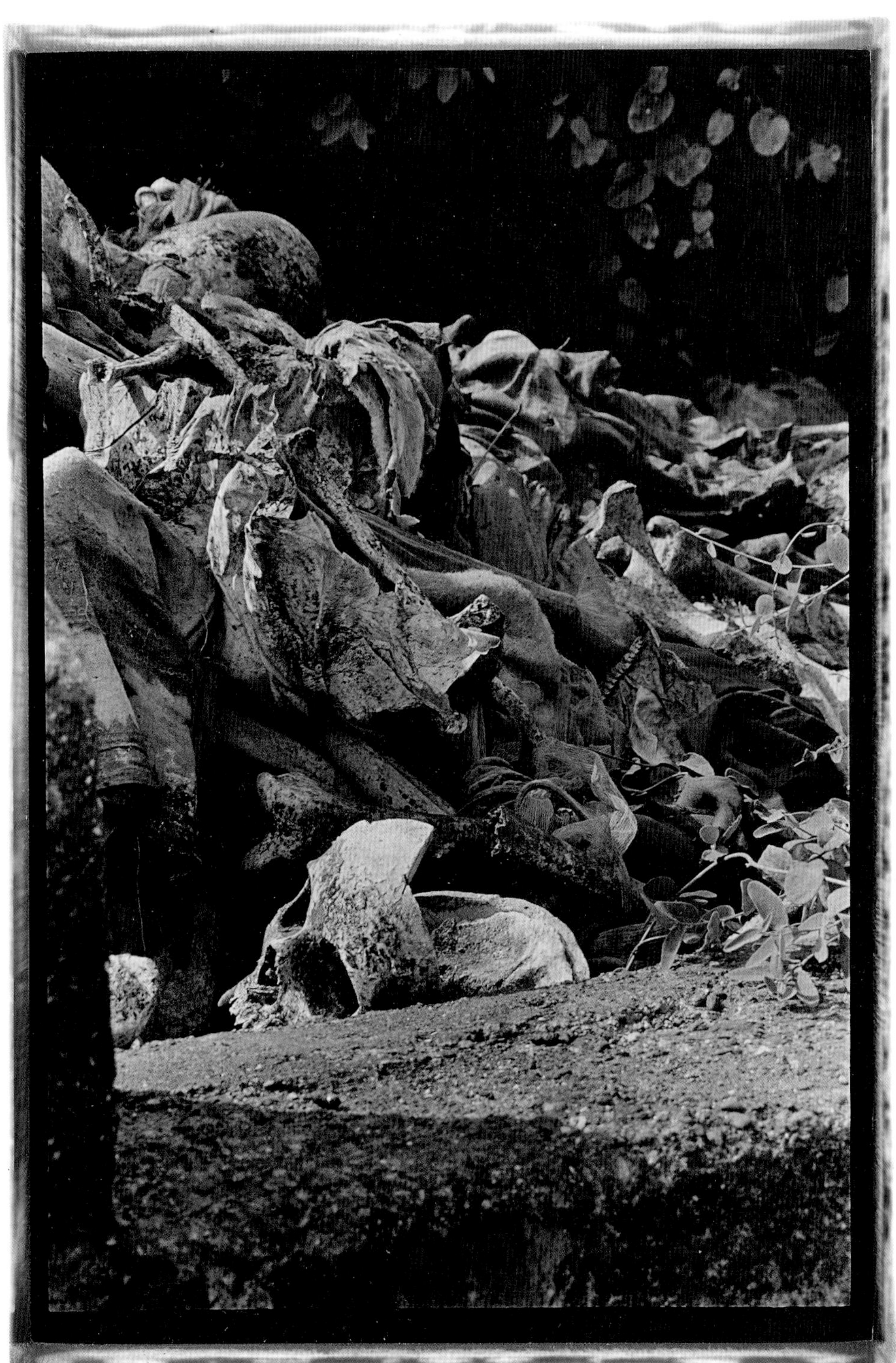

Vernon Fernandes

Graveyard at St. Andrew's Church,
Hill Road, Bandra.

*Whenever I go around the neighbourhood,
I know I can be out as long as I want,
I don't feel any fear.... I feel safe.*

Vernon Fernandes

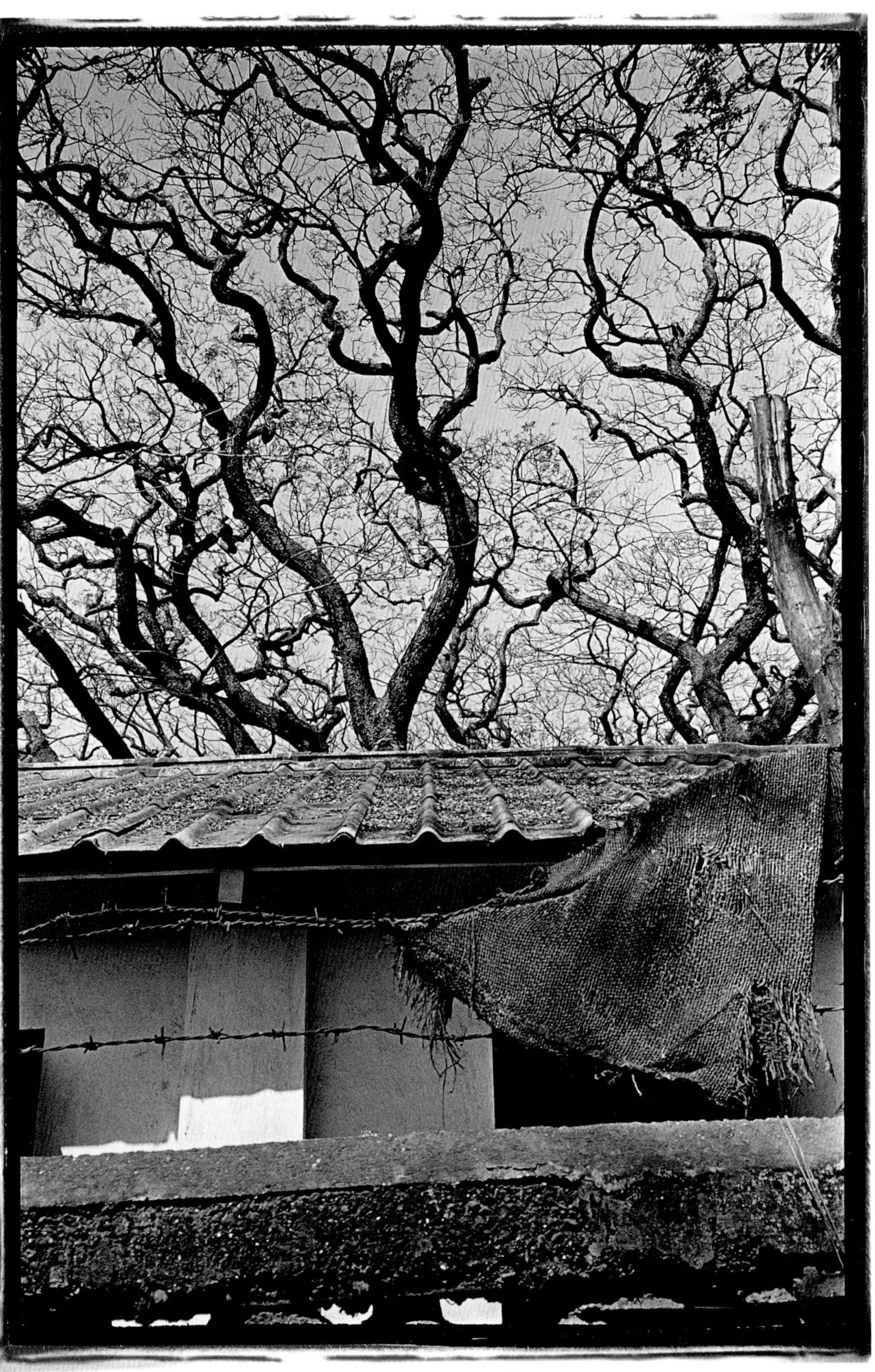

Anitha Balachandran
P. D'Mello Road, Umerkhadi.

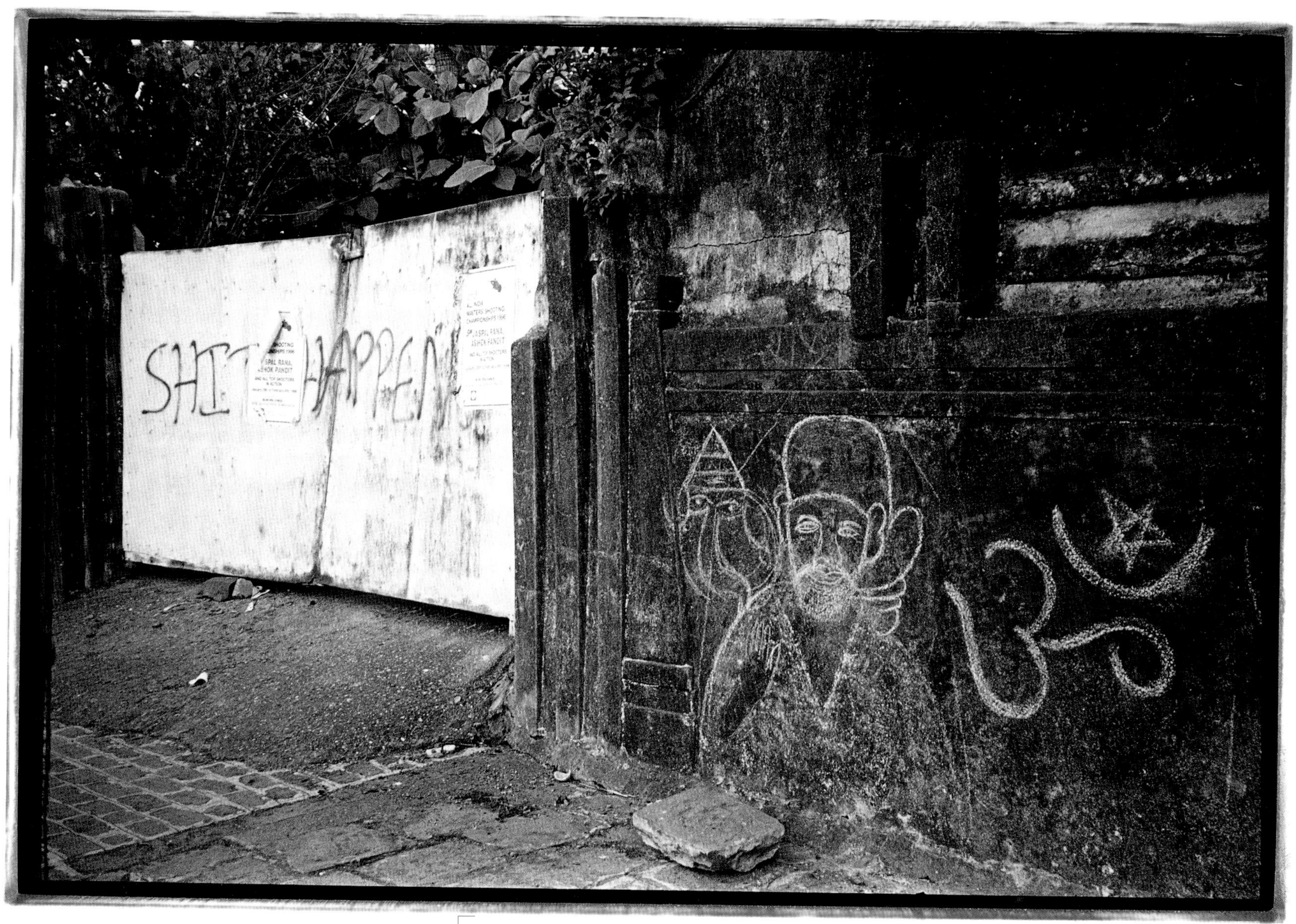

Nivedita Magar

Worli Sea Face, Maulana Abdul Gaffarkhan Road.

माझ्यासमोर उभे असलेले मुंबईचे चित्र म्हणजे सांस्कृतिक एकात्मता. इथे सर्व जातींच्या आणि धर्माच्या लोकांचा मानवतारूपी धर्मात मिलाफ झालेला आहे.

या शहराचा जिवंतपणा, भव्य इमारती आणि सर्व तऱ्हेची प्रगती या नगरातला एक लहानसा हिस्सा असलेल्या सामान्य माणसाला सुद्धा यशाचा हव्यास लावते.

इमारतींभोवती वेढलेल्या झोपडपट्ट्या भविष्यात राहतील किंवा नाही ते सांगता येत नाही. कारण मी पाहतोय की शहरामध्ये झपाट्याने बदल होतोय.

श्रीमंतांच्या दृष्टीने मुंबईतील राहणीमान सोपे आणि ऐषारामी आहे. परंतु गरिबांच्या दृष्टीने मात्र दिवस काढणे अतिशय कष्टदायक आहे.

मुंबईच्या आसपास असलेल्या स्मारकांकडे जनतेचे दुर्लक्ष होत आहे. भविष्यात ते टिकतील की नाही या विषयी मला शंका वाटते.

The picture of Mumbai that I have is one of cultural unity. People of all castes and religions seem to merge into a single religion of humanity.

The huge buildings and all the development don't seem to stop the common man from wanting success. He may be a small part of the whole city but the liveliness of the city pushes every person to reach for what he wants and to keep moving on and on.

The slums that seem to embrace all buildings may or may not be here in the long run, because I see the city changing. This is a temporary phase. The rich might find living in Mumbai easy and luxurious but the poor have a terrible time moving on.

The old monuments in and around Mumbai have been neglected by the people. I wonder whether in the future they may be there at all.

Sachin Sawant

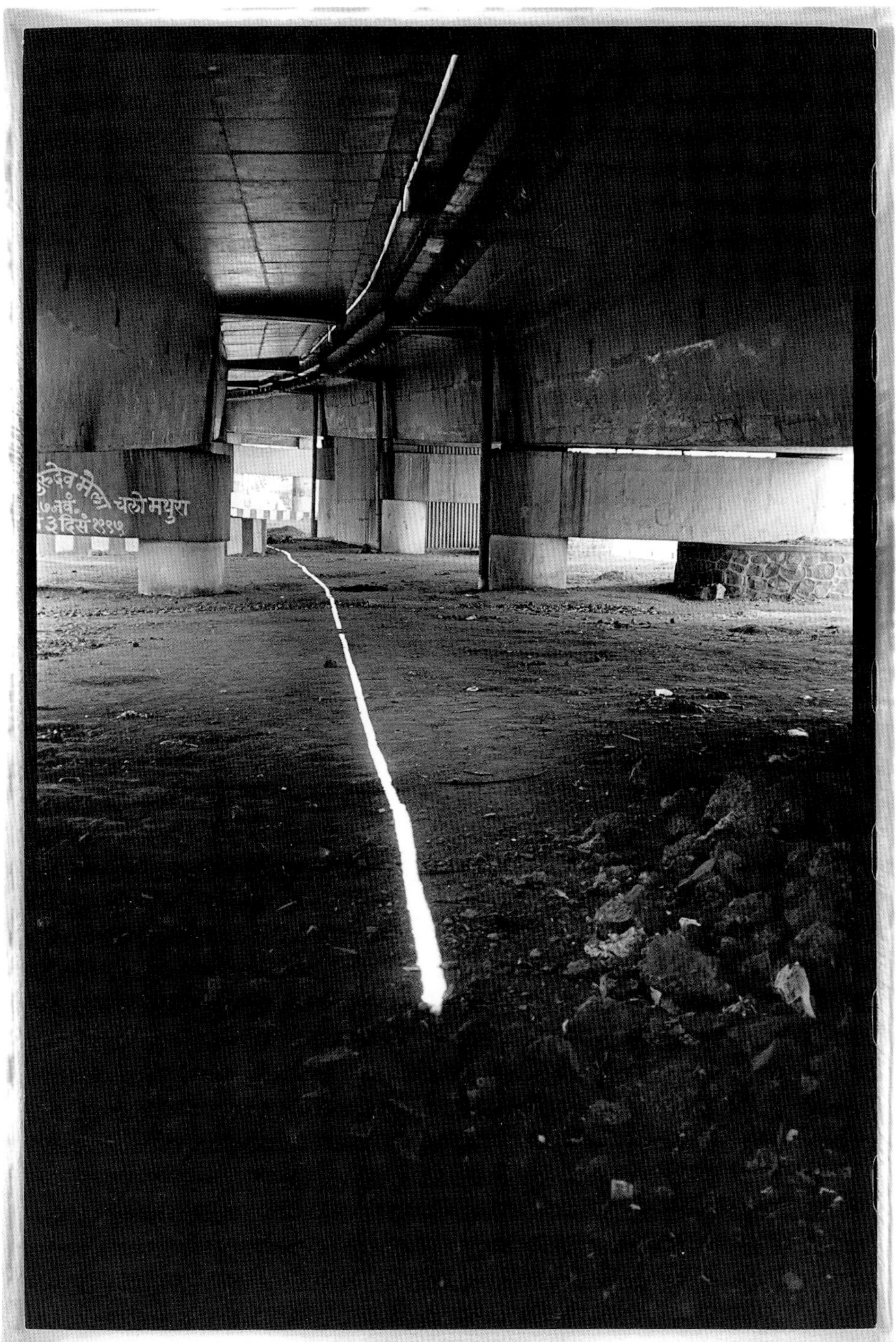

Vernon Fernandes
Kala Nagar Fly-over, Bandra.

... movement or change is a landmark to me. Crowds at the station, posters on a wall, or tyre marks on the road. The faces, the posters, and the tyre prints are always changing—but they are always there.

It is something I recognise Mumbai by. Something that gives me a sense of belonging, that I can take for granted. Dependable. A landmark waits for you day after day.

Anitha Balachandran

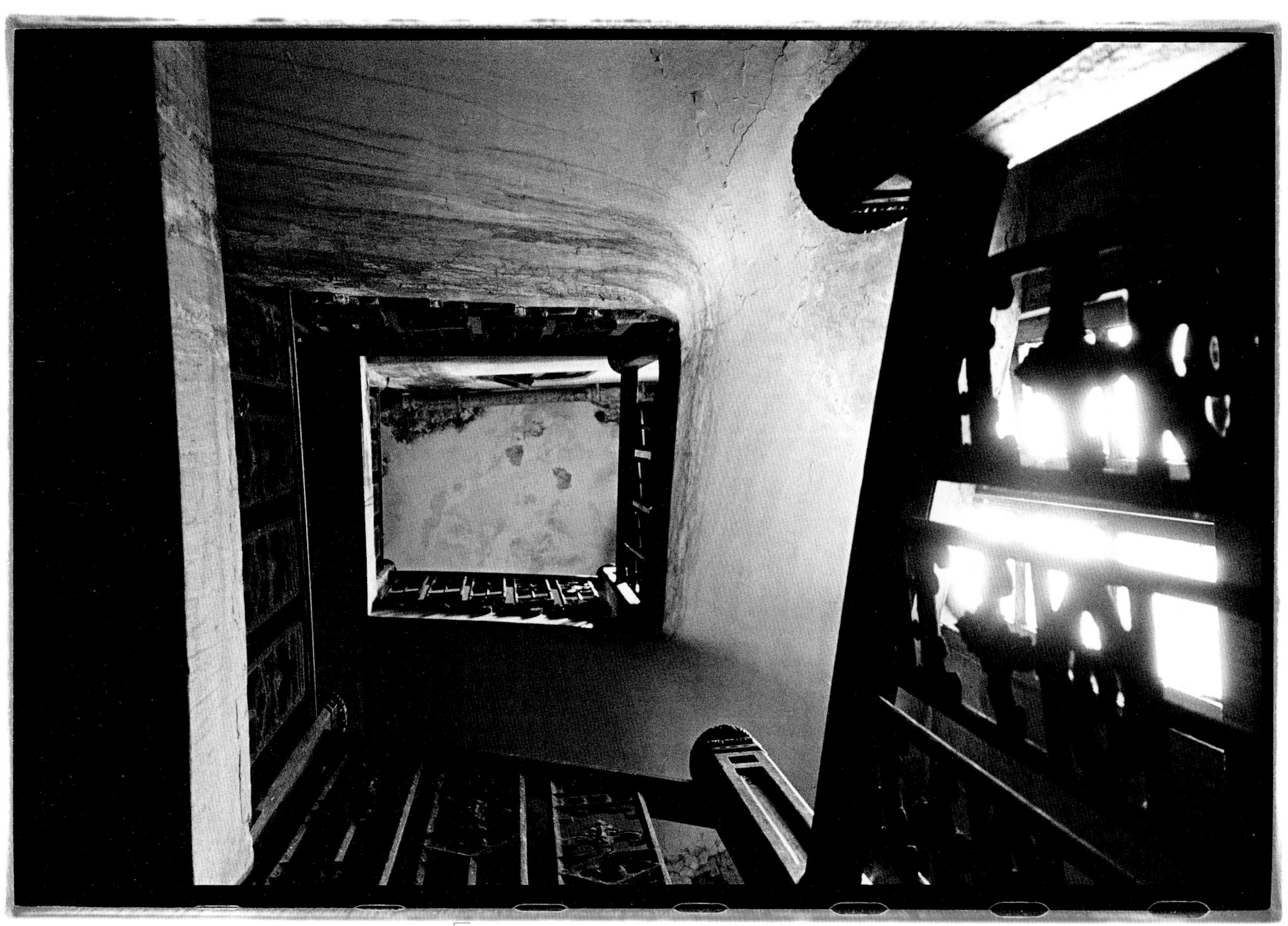

Nicole D'Souza
St. Xavier's College, Mahapalika Marg.

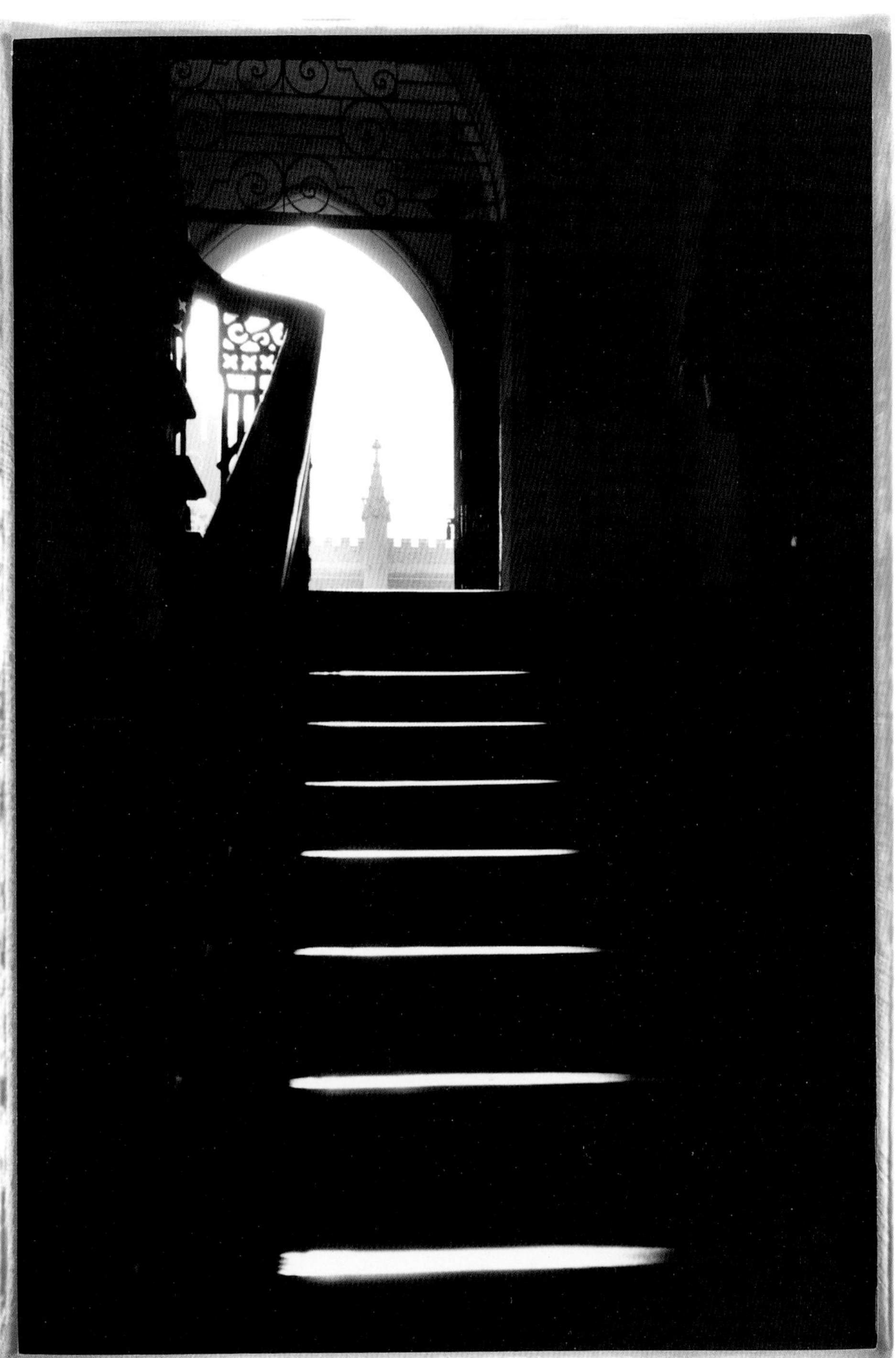

Nivedita Magar

St. Xavier's College, Mahapalika Marg.

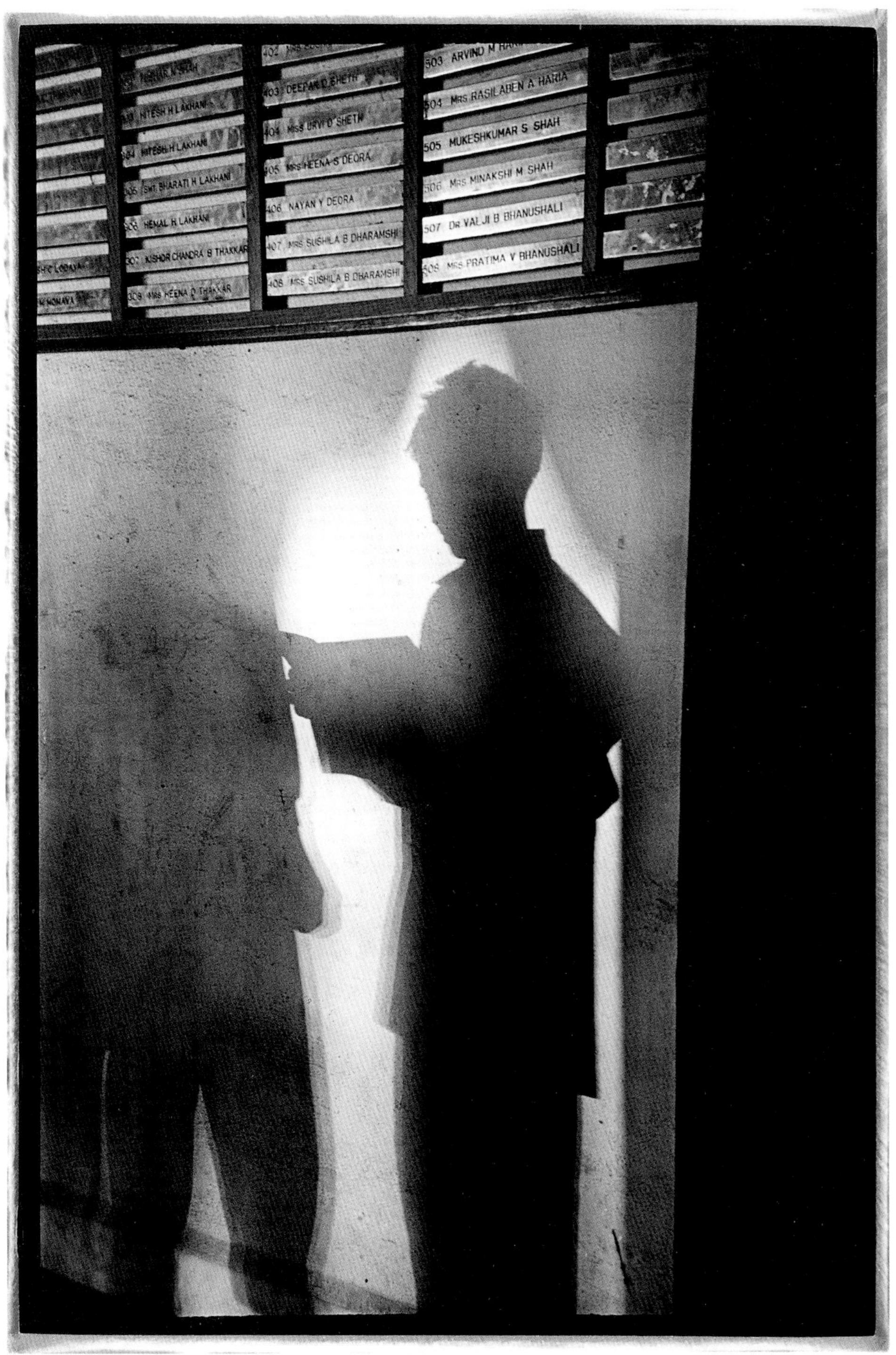

Vinit Chauhan
Vinit's building, Mulund.

My image of Bombay is closely linked with my perception of life. I think of the city as the context that I'm in, the backdrop for my act.

I think of Bombay as an integral part of me. For me to talk about it I shall have to step out of myself, and at 18 I'm afraid I'm not Buddha enough to do that. What I feel for the city is either too obscure to verbalise or perhaps too deep to access.

If I have to think of a city, especially a large urban metropolis like Bombay, things get awfully bigtime and unmanageable. Bombay to me is strangely not bigtime but a collage of little explosions... a bandaged bitch at Byculla station; the atrocity of the M. J. Concert; weighed down by humanity in the ladies' first-class compartment at rush hour; the B.J.P; a movie by Anand Patwardhan; a photograph; boom, boom, all around my head, Bombay deafens me sometimes till I'm numb. I saw a bloody corpse on the station and all that struck me was, what a lot of flies.

Stations in Bombay seem to be microcosms of the city at large. As the train pulls into the platform you can visibly tell the stratification in society, the working class, the professionals, the students, the smarty-pants with no tickets, and the ubiquitous vendor who tries to make a life selling anything, anywhere to anyone.

About photography—Everything does look better in black and white. Trust me, I know.

Nivedita Magar

> I believe life in Bombay is best when you don't watch out for it.

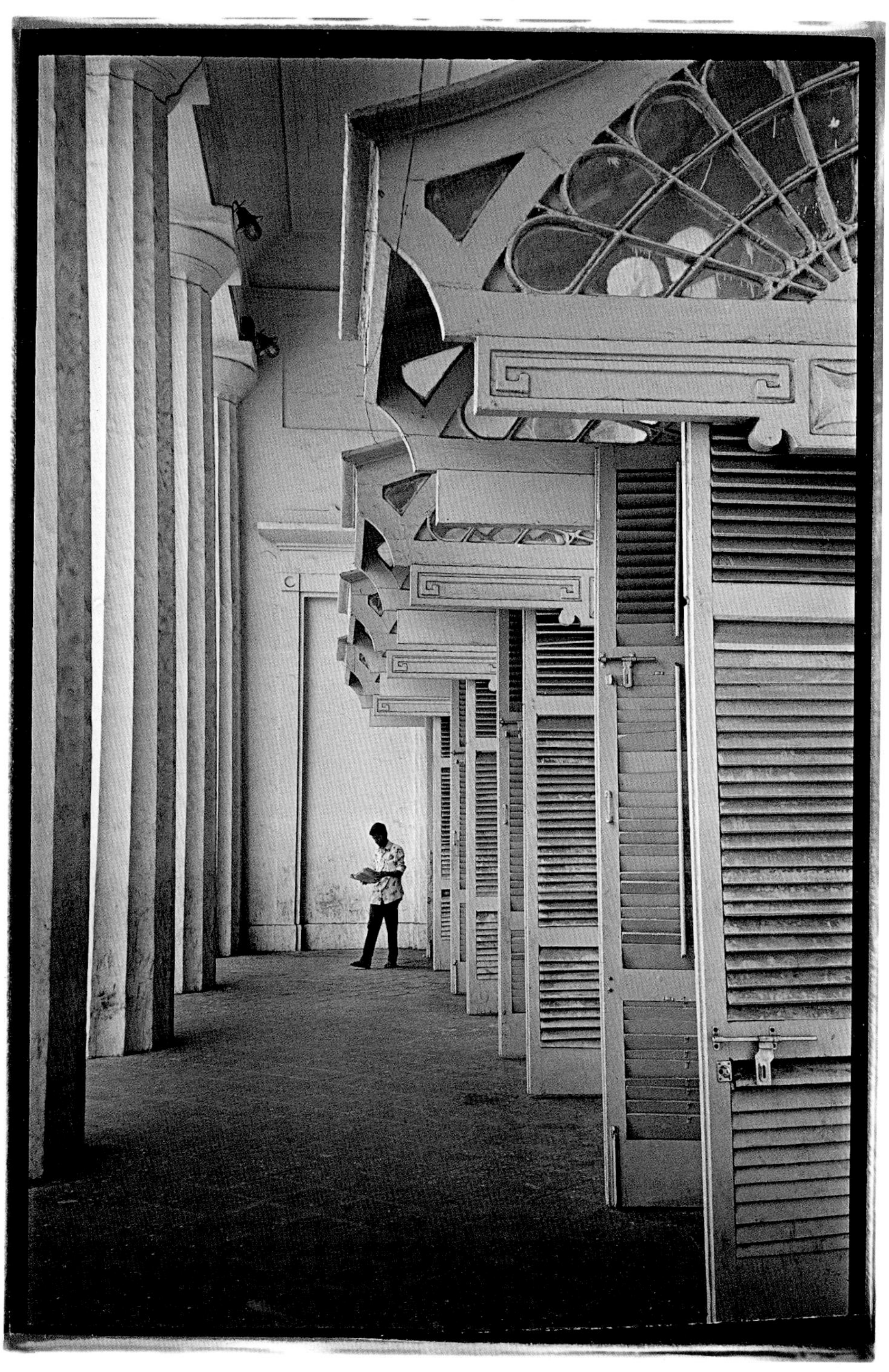

Anitha Balachandran
Asiatic Library, Horniman Circle,
Shahid Bhagatsingh Road.

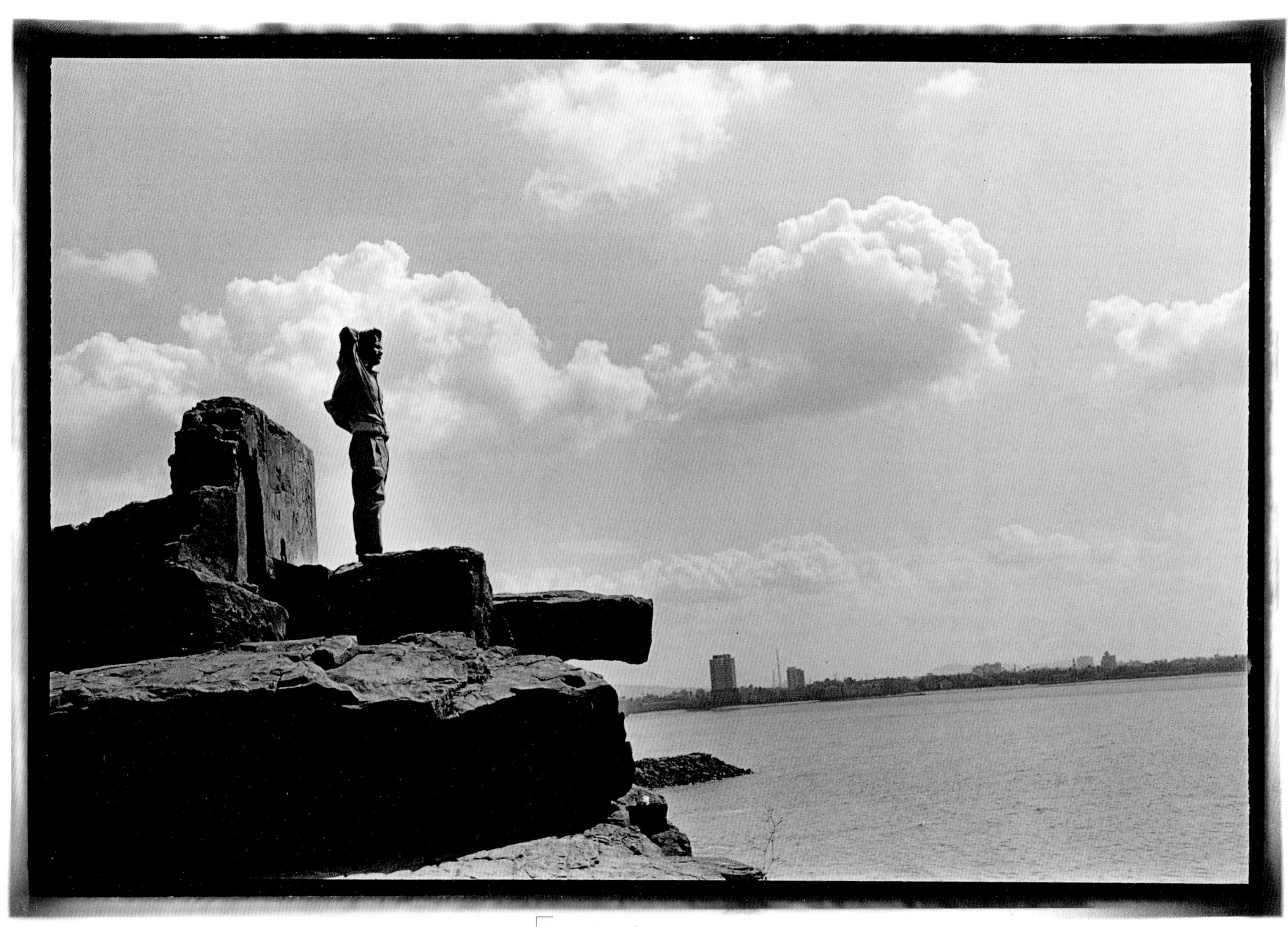

Vernon Fernandes
Land's End, Bandra.

When Mahasti Afshar enthusiastically selected Mumbai as one of the five cities in the world to participate in the Getty Conservation Institute project, there was considerable jubilation in our team which quickly changed to trepidation at the realisation of what seemed an impossible task; producing a pictorial documentary to infuse a sense of future.

Mumbai is a city that bears mute testimony to neglect and apathy. Where King Chaos reigns supreme. Ask a Mumbaiite (a denizen of the city) what could be worth conserving for all posterity and the response most likely would be an incredulous look. This city, with a rich and eventful past, often seems to have no future; the ebb and flow of humanity in its streets, homes, and offices, intent on survival at all costs, reflect only the urgency of the day. This is compounded by the fact that vast numbers of people share a multiplicity of languages and religions. How then were we to identify the elements that unify us all?

Nine young people of this city, who had placed eye to camera, should dispel all such doubts. Through this body of work, unfettered by a jaundiced adult viewpoint, they have perhaps unwittingly yet unerringly distilled the essence of life in this city and offered every Mumbaiite the power to embrace the familiar. The sights, sounds, and smells of Mumbai are faithfully embedded within the graphic beauty of each black and white image; freeze frames that would serve to change the perspective, give pause for reflection, and provide the bedrock on which to anchor our identities.

It has been a cathartic experience for all of us who have been involved in bringing this project to fruition. The process as powerful as the product. Walking through schools and obtaining permissions from homes, realisation dawned that we had been oblivious to the quiet existence of teachers who love and parents who teach. They are there, unknown to all except those they touch, imbibing the values of our heritage and instilling a vision of a future in their wards; conservationists in their own right. The Getty Conservation Institute's efforts through this project have catalysed dreams in all of us of perpetuating this process. Plans have been drawn up to take the show on the road and several spirited souls in other Indian cities have shown great interest in propagating the idea. Nine children could be ninety or even nine million. This is just the beginning.

Efforts such as this one sponsored by the GCI play an invaluable role in fostering an understanding of, and consequently respect for, the unique values and ways of nations and their peoples. There are several such initiatives in progress from within our country too, some extremely successful. Often started by an individual with no more than a dream and an irrepressible urge to reach out and make a difference.

Such considerations drew me to contribute what I could towards this ideal. This tired and aging city, its streets and alleyways, its clustered communes, has been home. She has moulded me in more ways than I could know. Not unlike so many other cities in our nation, indeed around the world, it needs all the help it can get. There is an urgency that raises a clarion call for Corporate India to marshall its resources, using them proactively and imaginatively. After all, can there be a global village without a global community?

When the GCI initiated "Picture L.A." no one had imagined the startling impact it would have on all the participants. "Picture Mumbai" mirrored that experience as, no doubt, will the other cities slated to run the project. As each of their stories unfolds, it should become increasingly apparent that, under the veneer of differences, they all remain our children. Our responsibility. Our future.

Anil Rao
Project Manager

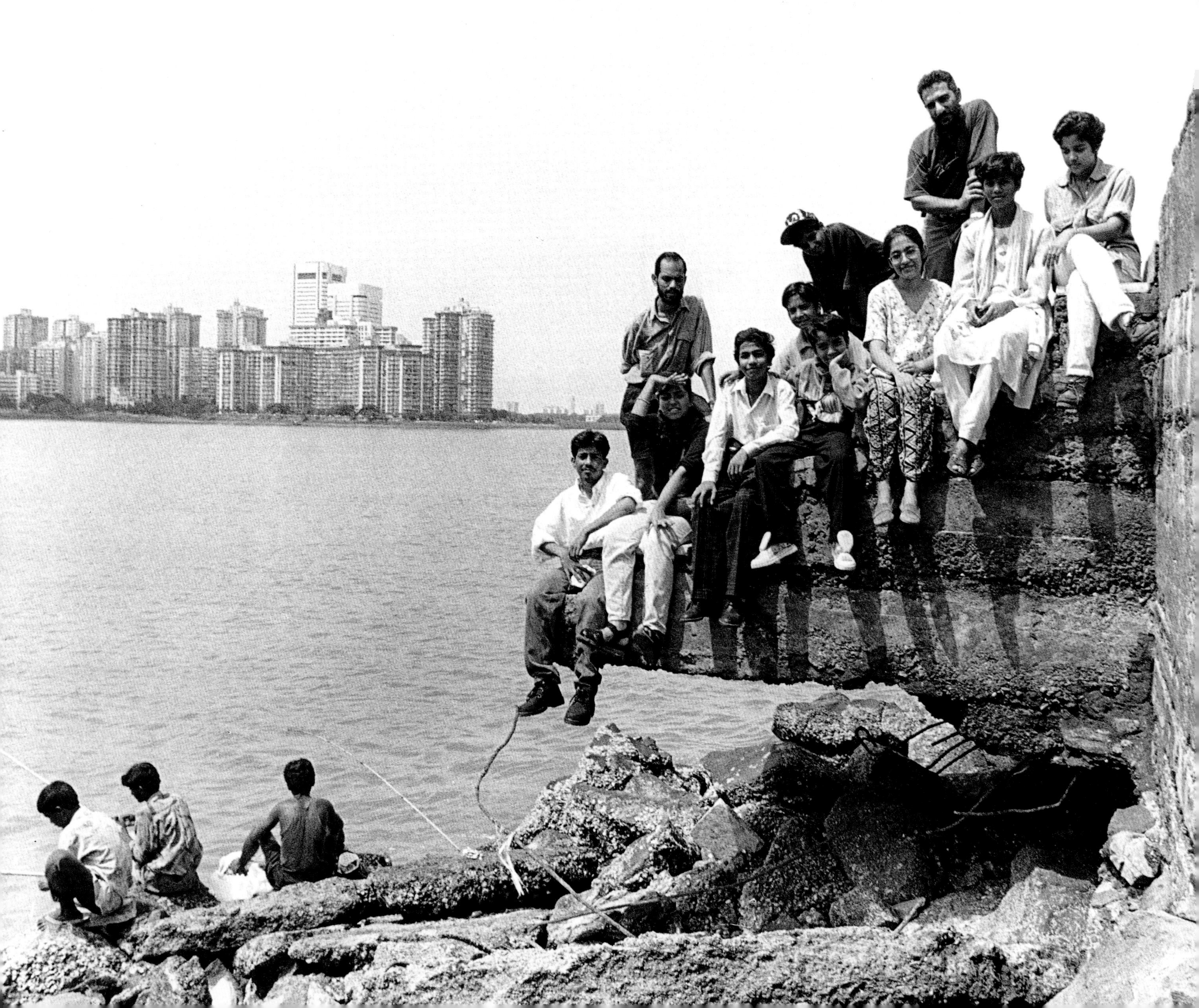

At twelve last January he is the youngest and physically the smallest in the group. He lives with his parents and a younger brother in a northern suburb (Bhandup). Asir goes to the Shivai School very close to where he lives. He has a fully developed personality and can hold his own without being

Asir Mulla

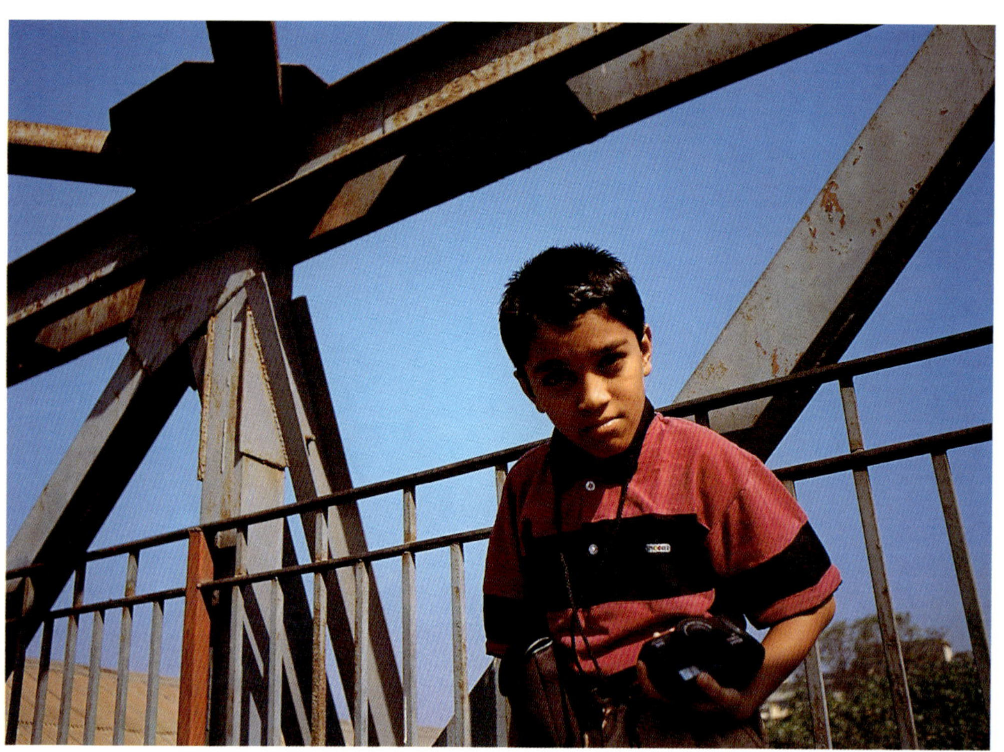

precocious. He is totally vernacular, is a Muslim, speaks Marathi at home, is unafraid to ask questions. He has loads of self confidence and represents the Mumbai that has attitude. He loves the project. Is totally beguiling. Adults cannot but acquiesce when he asks to photograph them.

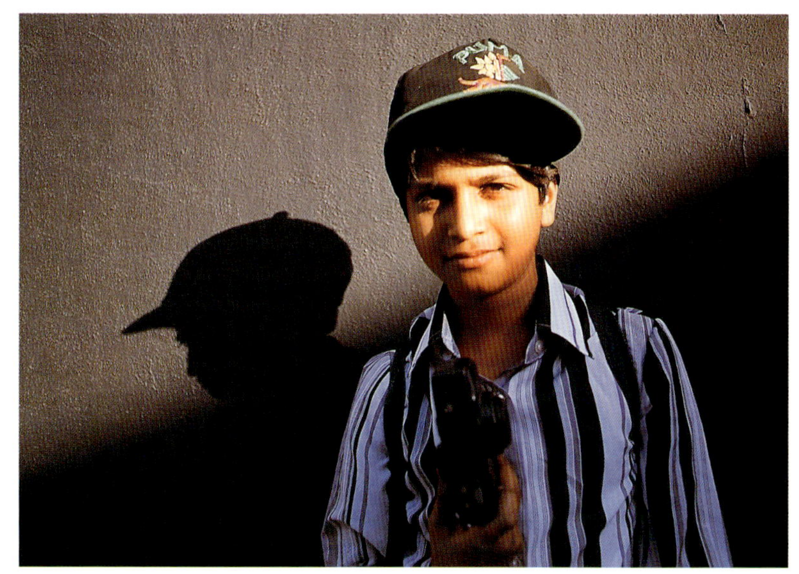

Twelve years old, lives with his parents in the very East Indian, Christian neighbourhood of Bandra, has a much older brother who is a sailor. He goes to St. Stanislaus High School. Vernon stood out in the school interview because of his original views and cool confidence. He is the most mischievous in the group and is constantly teasing the girls. He also happens to be the most chivalrous and accident prone. Is full of energy and ready to get to any precipice. This project has given him a terrific morale boost and is proving to his family and school that he is in every way valuable. He represents the restless Mumbai, the organism that never sleeps.

At fifteen is at the precarious final school examination stage. He lives with his mother and older brother in the cotton mill neighbourhood of Parel. He is sensitive, quiet, and very artistic, constantly playing with objects and juxtaposing them with light and squinting at the effects. He has a unique perspective. He went to the very progressive Shirodkar vernacular school for mill-worker children and feels his talents are being nurtured. He is now preparing himself for a formal education in the arts. He is excited to be in the project. He represents the tentative Mumbai.

Sachin Sawant

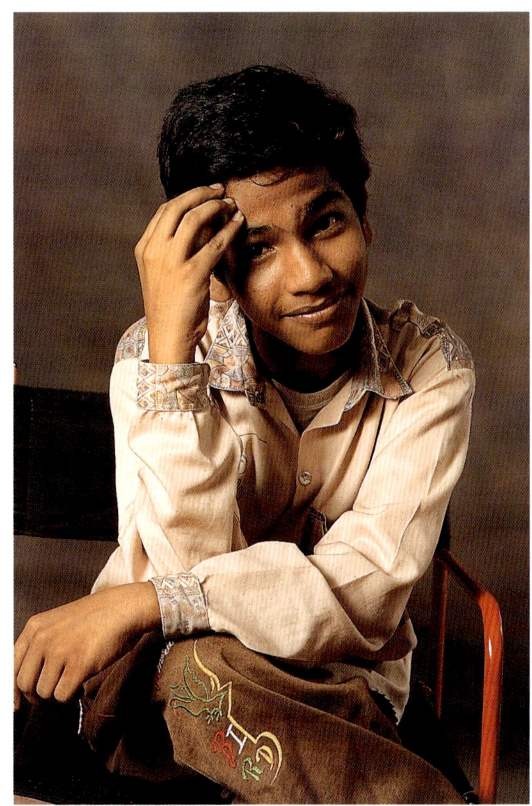

⌐Yamini Hule⌐

Is fifteen years old and was a contemporary of Sachin in the Shirodkar school at Parel. She is tall, athletic, affectionate, full of passion, excitement, and the joy of living. She has a sparkle in her eye and through her father's enlightened encouragement manages to get a broad spectrum of experiences. She speaks Marathi and is totally integrated. She is exceptionally bright, paints, plays competition chess, high jumps, is a distance runner, and represented her school in all these extra curricular activities. She lives not too far from the school with her parents. She is also interested in commercial art and is in training at the SNDT. She represents the versatile, all encompassing Mumbai. She is a joy to watch totally art directing her photographs. Like her running strategy her visuals were slow to start with but in full flow towards the end.

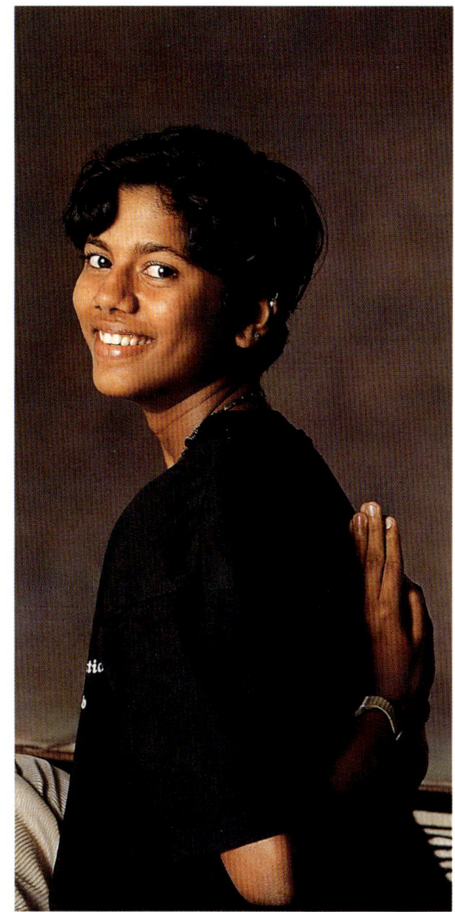

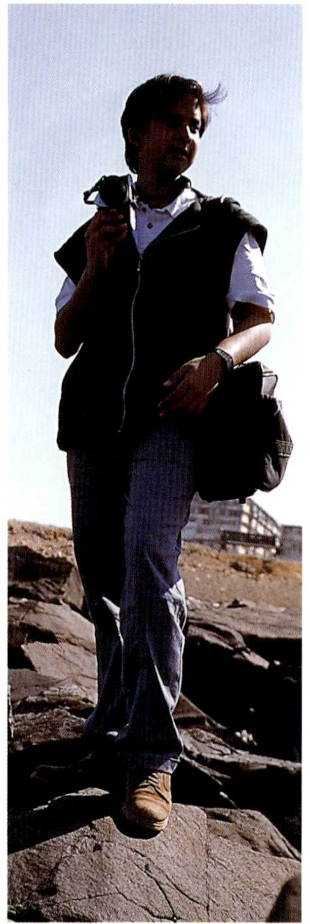

Bikram Mitra

Is fifteen years old, lives in the neighbourhood of Breach Candy, and goes to the Bombay International School in downtown Mumbai. He lost his mother recently in an auto accident, lives with his dad and younger brother. Bikram is the only young person in the group who has previous photo experience and insisted on using his single lens reflex. He was probably the most pressured person in the project balancing his studies for the final school examination from March 15, his father's very high expectations of him, and the obvious camaraderie and differentness of the project. At the moment he is in Jai Hind college. He is a shy, retiring sort of person with an oscillating desire to become a photographer. When he's with us he swings this way, presumably when he's with his Dad he will become a rocket scientist! He represents the other face of the proverbial brash Bombay (it wouldn't sound the same with "Mumbai").

Is seventeen years old. His parents died in an auto accident in Baroda in the neighbouring state of Gujarat. He became an instant orphan and decided to run away from an ill-treating uncle. He lived totally disoriented for a day on the platform of Victoria Terminus station. Luckily for him he was spotted the very next day by a voluntary organisation called Support that works with runaway street kids. Vinit has felt nurtured in the shelter and lives with other less fortunate kids. He is refined and his ambitions have led him to the J. D. Fashion Institute. He wears unique clothing and is fulfilling his desire to become a fashion designer. He is Hindi speaking, very quiet, nobody knows when and how he makes his beautiful images. The project has given him an opportunity to integrate democratically. He represents the all encompassing, all absorbing, mother Mumbai.

⌐Vinit Chauhan⌐

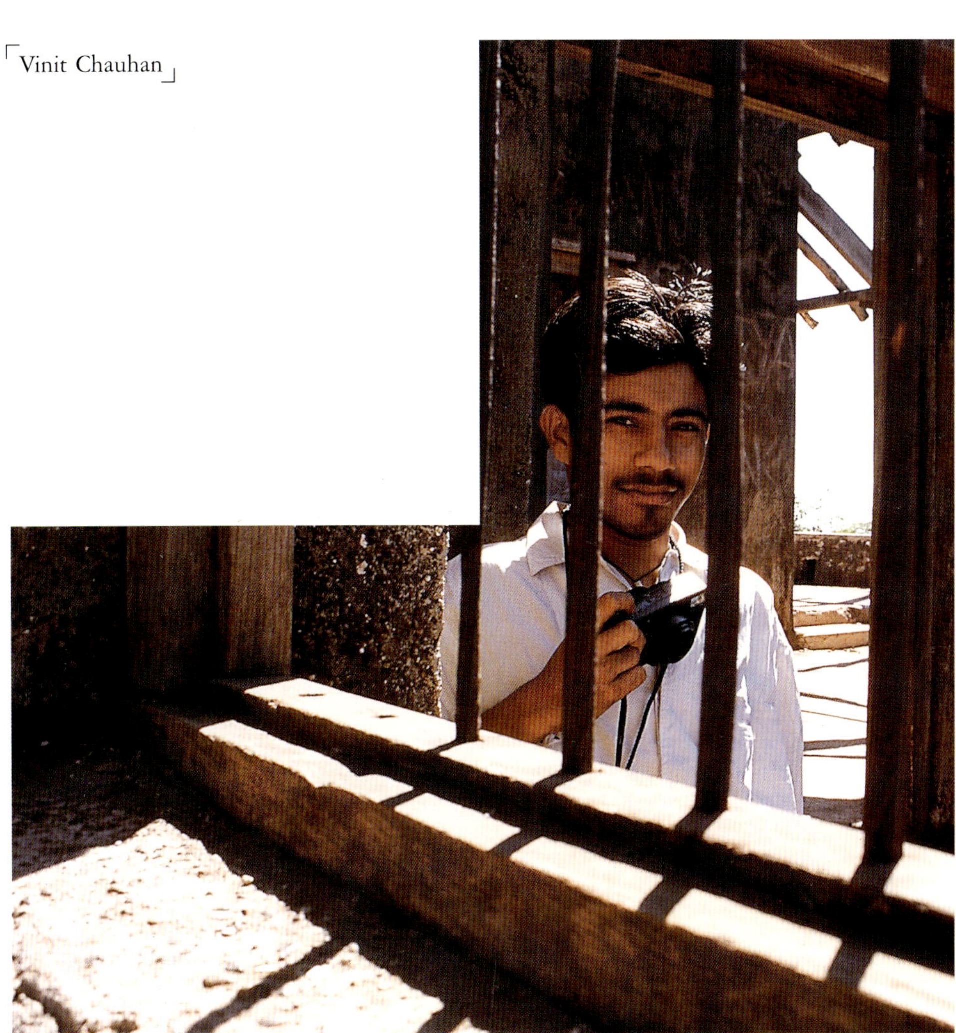

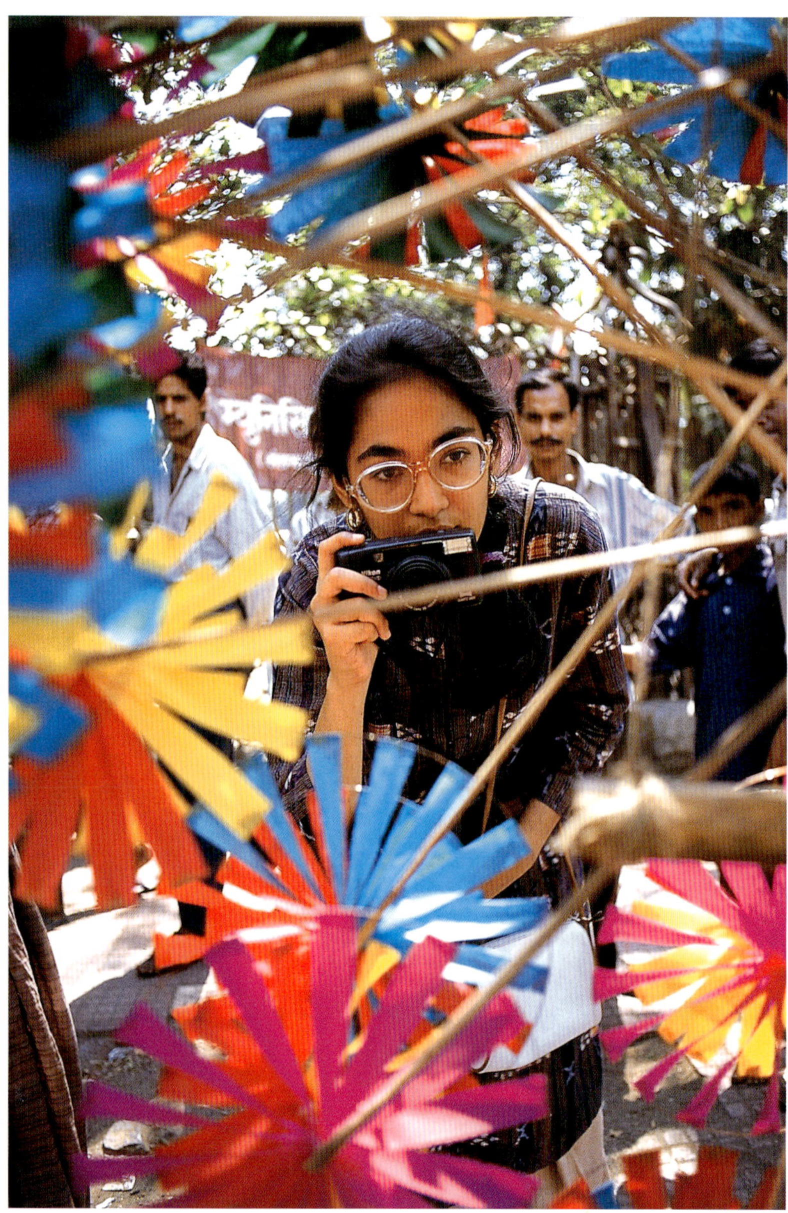

⌐Anitha Balachandran⌐

Is seventeen and lives with her parents who are on assignment in Mumbai. She, like Vinit, are relative newcomers to the city. She has lived here for a year and finds everything fascinating. She finds the people here more accepting and involving. She used to go to St. Xavier's College where she was pursuing a career in economics but was not quite convinced that she wanted her life to go that way. An opportunity to join the National Institute of Design convinced her to use her artistic talents in this field. Using the camera and black and white film for the first time she has found a unique voice with her images. She has a wonderful perspective, is cultured, soft spoken. She represents the sensitive Mumbai.

Is eighteen, goes to St. Xavier's College, and is pursuing a degree in Psychology and Literature. She lives with her parents and older sister in Kurla, a suburb of Mumbai. She is at the stage when "women's issues" and gender correctness form a backdrop to her thoughts. She finds the city's men folk irksome and wants to unleash her camera on them. She has some more interesting images of people and works her photographs. She is open, innocent, and thoughtful. She brings a beautiful perspective to the project. She says she lives for the weekends and is enjoying the experience. She represents the side of Mumbai rarely seen — insightful.

Nivedita Magar

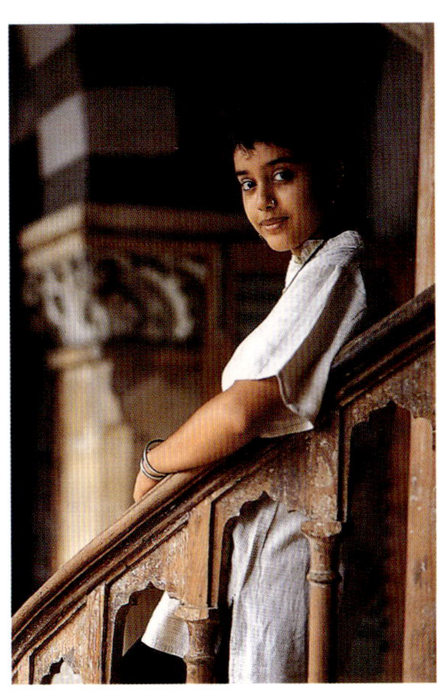

Nicole D'Souza

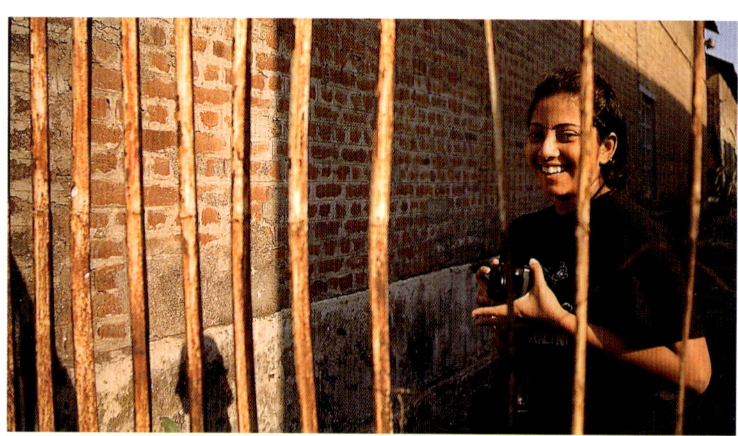

Is eighteen, also goes to St. Xavier's College, and is majoring in Psychology. She lives with her parents and sister in the central Mumbai region of Byculla. She is communicative, ready to hug everyone, belongs to a generation that idolises the likes of Bon Jovi and Aerosmith. She makes visual statements on loneliness in this overpopulated city. She represents the gregarious Mumbai.

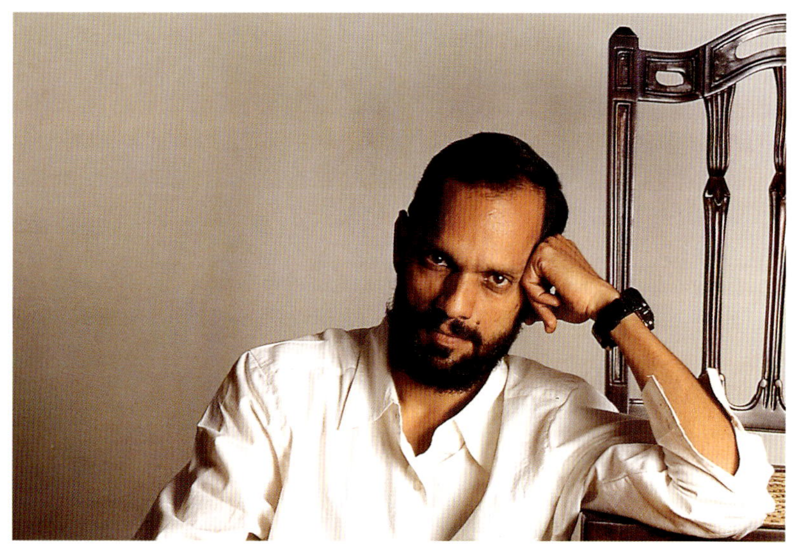

David de Souza

Started out his working life as a biochemist where he lectured at G.S. Medical College. He moved to Petroleum Chemistry with the Arabian American Oil Co. in Saudi Arabia. In addition to chemistry he did the company's industrial/corporate photography. He knew when he bought his first camera in 1977 that this is where he wanted to go. He has been a professional photographer since 1989 doing advertising photography. He does not know why or how he got the "Picture Mumbai" project, but feels that nothing better could have happened to him. He prefers to express himself through photography as a fine art, and much prefers the photo essayist genre. He is working on a couple of books and is an outdoors person. His newest area of concern is setting up a self sustainable trust to encourage the visual arts.

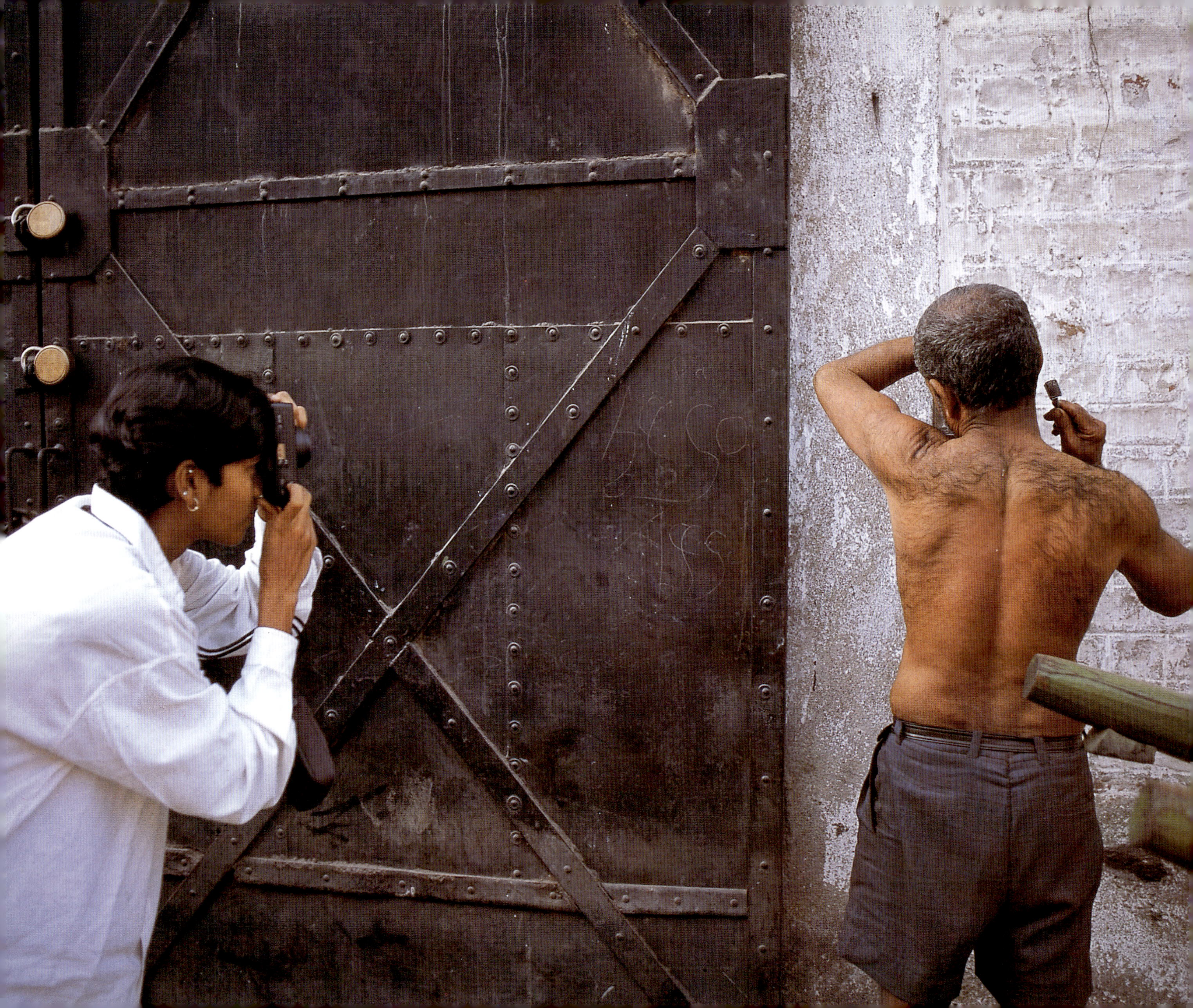

PROJECT PARTICIPANTS

CONCEPT:

Miguel Angel Corzo

PROJECT DIRECTOR:

Mahasti Afshar

PROJECT MANAGER:

Anil Rao

FIELD DIRECTOR:

David de Souza

ASSISTANTS:

Nuzhat Khan

Sachin Chitale

Suresh Dhadve

PHOTOGRAPHY:

Asir Mulla

Vernon Fernandes

Sachin Sawant

Yamini Hule

Bikram Mitra

Vinit Chauhan

Anitha Balachandran

Nivedita Magar

Nicole D'souza

CATALOGUE:

Designer:
Sunil Mahadik
FX Designs, Mumbai.

Processing:
Unique Photo-Offset Services
Mumbai.

Printing:
Pragati Art Printers
Hyderabad.

Photo Editing Consultant:
Dr. Hemant Morparia

EXHIBITION:

Design And Execution:
R. J. B. Design
Mumbai.

EXHIBITION PRINTS:

X.IBIT
Los Angeles, California.

CO-ORDINATORS:

Vinod Daniel

Anita Keys

VIDEO:

Producer/Director/Camera:
David de Souza

PUBLIC INFORMATION:

Los Angeles:
Lori Starr

Cynthia Wornham

Libby Rogers

Mumbai:
Mid-Day Publications Ltd.

ACKNOWLEDGEMENTS

The participants of "Picture Mumbai" wish to thank the following for their assistance and support.

Dr. Kalpana Desai
Director, Prince of Wales Museum of Western India.

Dr. P. C. Alexander
Governor, State of Maharashtra.

Fr. Emile D'Cruz
Principal, St. Xavier's College

Fr. Terence Quadros
Counsellor, St. Xavier's College

Fr. Edmund Carasco
Principal, St. Stanislaus High School

Dr. Sanjeev Gandhi

Ms. Sujata Ganega
Director, "SUPPORT"

Mr. Sadashiv Bhoir

Mr. Vishwas Dhumal
Principal, Shivai Vidya Mandir

Mr. Sambajirao Sonavane
Principal, Dr. Shirodkar High School

Mr. Parshuram Nabar

Mr. Ramdas Shirke

Mrs. M. Ramadurai
Vice Principal, Bombay International High School

Ms. Christodas

Mr. Amir Khan

Ms. Louise D'Costa

Mr. Vivek Boppaiah

Mrs. Tina Boppaiah

Mrs. Charmayne D'Souza

Mumbai Port Trust

Pest Control (India) Ltd.

Mr. Rakesh Kumar

Mr. William Parker
Director, USIS, *New Delhi.*

Mr. Joseph Brennig
Director, USIS, *Mumbai.*

Mr. Rajiv Agarwal

Mr. Achyut Palav

Mr. Vinay Patil

Mr. Vijay Sawant

Mr. M. S. Khan

Mr. Sebastian Coutinho

PARENTS

Mr. & Mrs. Mulla

Mr. & Mrs. Fernandes

Mrs. Sawant

Mr. & Mrs. Hule

Dr. Mitra

Mr. & Mrs. Balachandran

Dr. & Mrs. Magar

Mr. & Mrs. D'Souza